Collingwood Ontario in Photos, Saving Our History One Photo at a Time

Photography
by Barbara Raué
2013

Series Name:
Cruising Ontario

Book 28: Collingwood

Cover photo: Collingwood Grain Elevator

Series Name: Cruising Ontario

Book 1: London
Book 2: Dundas
Book 3: Hamilton
Book 4: Oakville
Book 5: Chesley
Book 6: Stoney Creek
Book 7: Waterdown
Book 8: Owen Sound
Book 9: Mount Forest
Book 10: Dundalk
Book 11: Burford and Area
Book 12: Waterford and Area
Book 13: Drumbo and Area
Book 14: Sheffield and Area
Book 15: Tavistock and Area
Book 16: Ancaster and Mount Hope
Book 17: Innerkip
Book 18: Brantford
Book 19: Burlington
Book 20: Guelph and Area
Book 21: Ayr
Book 22: Erin
Book 23: Goderich
Book 24: Lucknow and Area
Book 25: Paris and Glen Morris
Book 26: Toronto
Book 27: Beaver Valley
Book 28: Collingwood
Book 29: Peterborough
Book 30: Orangeville Beginnings Part 1
Book 31: Orangeville Part 2 and Area
Book 32: Port Elgin

Other Books by Barbara Raue

Coins of Gold

Arrows, Indians and Love

The Life and Times of Barbara
Volume 1: Inventions That Have Enhanced My Life
Volume 2: Entertainment That I Have Enjoyed
Volume 3: East Coast Trips
Volume 4: Olympics Have Always Intrigued Me
Volume 5: Wonders of the World
Volume 6: Caribbean Cruises We Have Enjoyed
Volume 7: Animals
Volume 8: Storms and Other Major Disasters in My Lifetime
Volume 9: Wars, Terrorist Attacks and Major Disasters

The Cromwell Family Book

Visit Barbara's website to view all of her books
http://barbararaue.ericraue.com

Collingwood

Collingwood is situated on Nottawasaga Bay at the southern point of Georgian Bay. Collingwood offers a combination of old time charm and history with recreation opportunities for skiing on Blue Mountain, and golfing.

Collingwood was incorporated as a town in 1858, nine years before Confederation and was named after Admiral Lord Cuthbert Collingwood, Lord Nelson's second in command at the Battle of Trafalgar, who assumed command of the British fleet after Nelson's death.

The land in the area was originally inhabited by the Iroquoian Petun nation, which built a string of villages in the vicinity of the nearby Niagara Escarpment. They were driven from the region by the Iroquois in 1650. European settlers and freed black slaves arrived in the area in the 1840s, bringing with them their religion and culture.

In 1855, the Ontario, Simcoe & Huron (later called The Northern) railway came into Collingwood, and the harbour became the place for shipment of goods destined for the upper Great Lakes ports of Chicago and Port Arthur-Ft. William (now Thunder Bay). Shipping produced a need for ship repairs, so it was not long before an organized ship building business was created. On May 24, 1883, the Collingwood Shipyards, formerly known as Collingwood Dry Dock Shipbuilding and Foundry Company Limited, opened with a special ceremony. On September 12, 1901, the Huronic was launched in Collingwood, the first steel-hulled ship launched in Canada. The shipyards produced Lakers and during World War II contributed to the production of Corvettes for the Royal Canadian Navy. Shipbuilding was one of the principal industries in the town, employing as much as 10% of the total labour force. Overseas competition and over capacity in shipbuilding in Canada led to the demise of shipbuilding in Collingwood in September 1986.

Collingwood to attract eleven new manufacturing firms to the town by 1971. Eight additional manufacturing companies had located in the town by 1983, making Collingwood the largest industrial employer in the region.

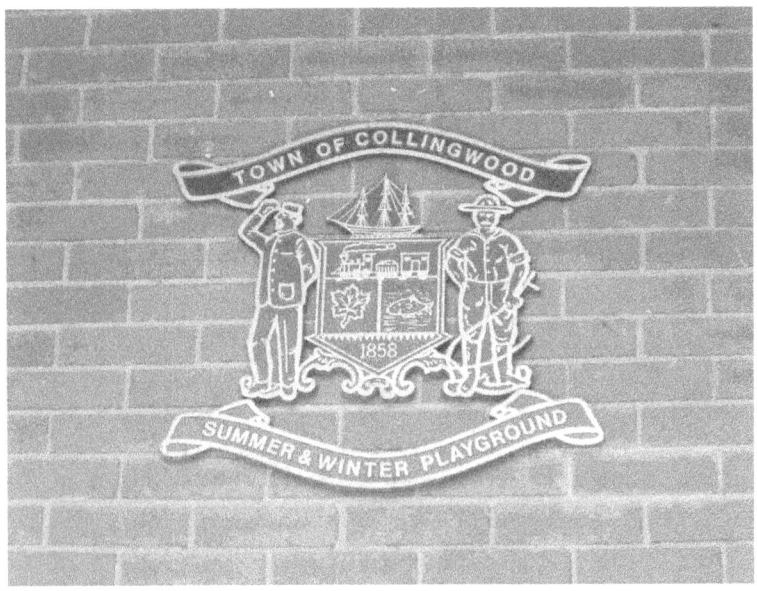

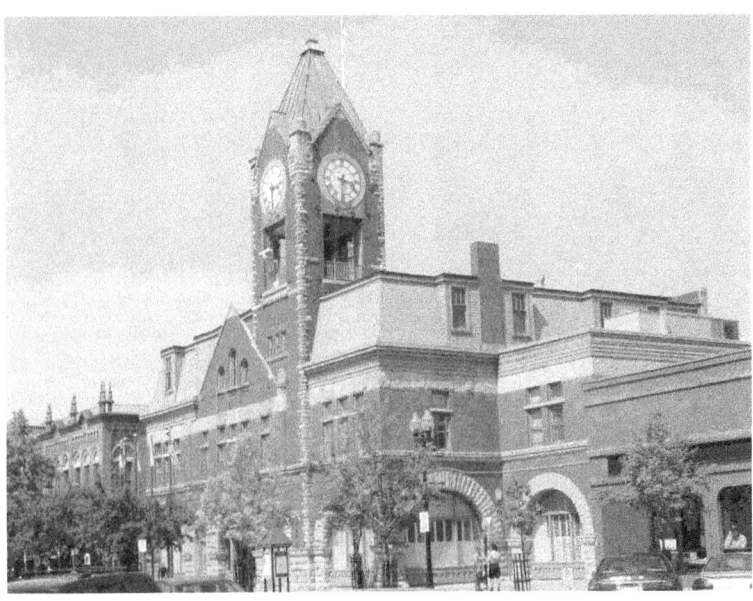

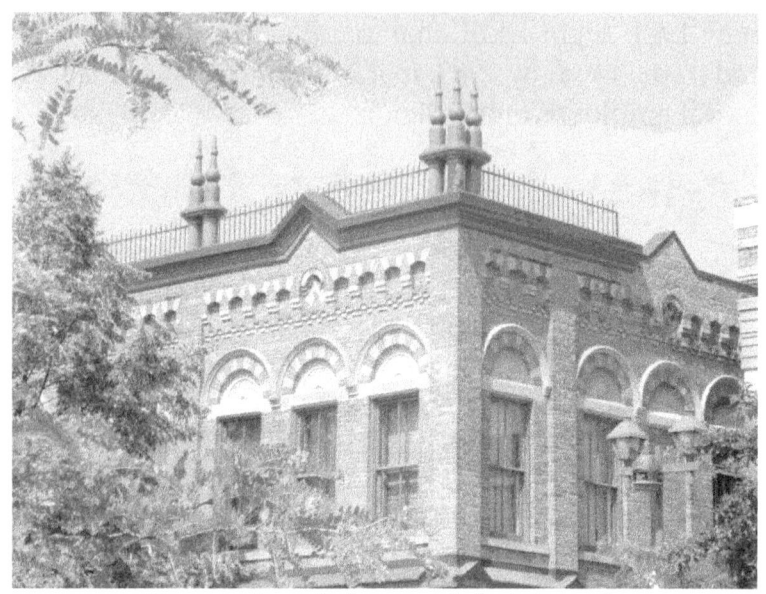
Decorative dichromatic brickwork

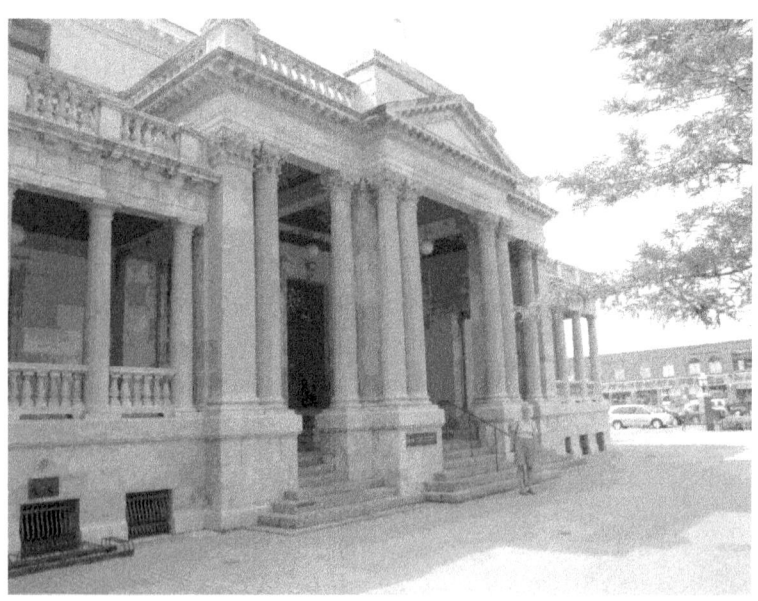

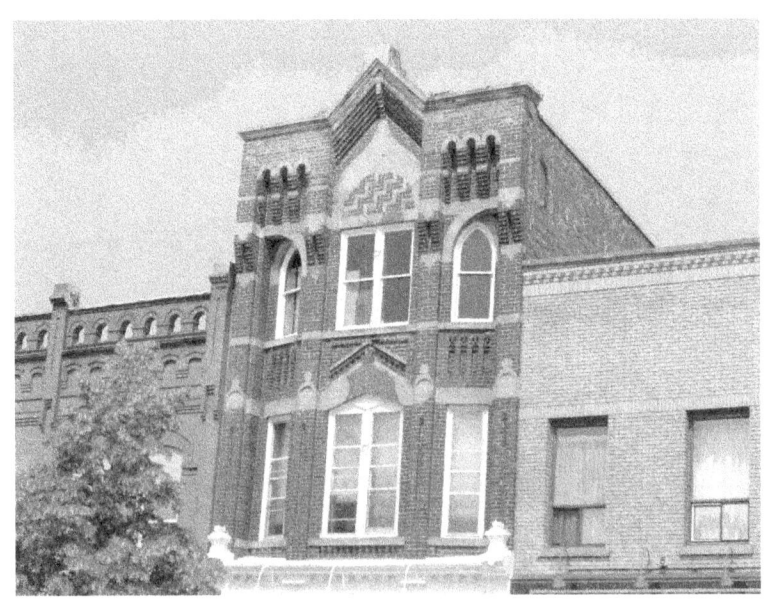

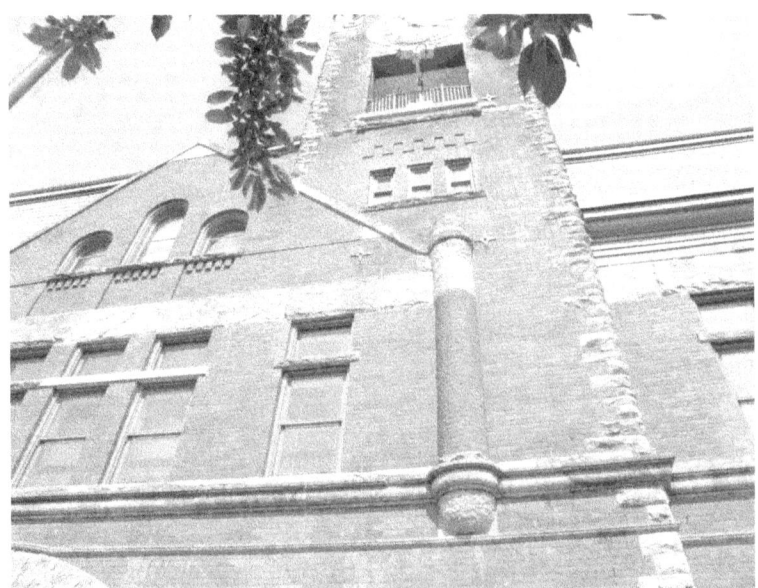

Corner quoins

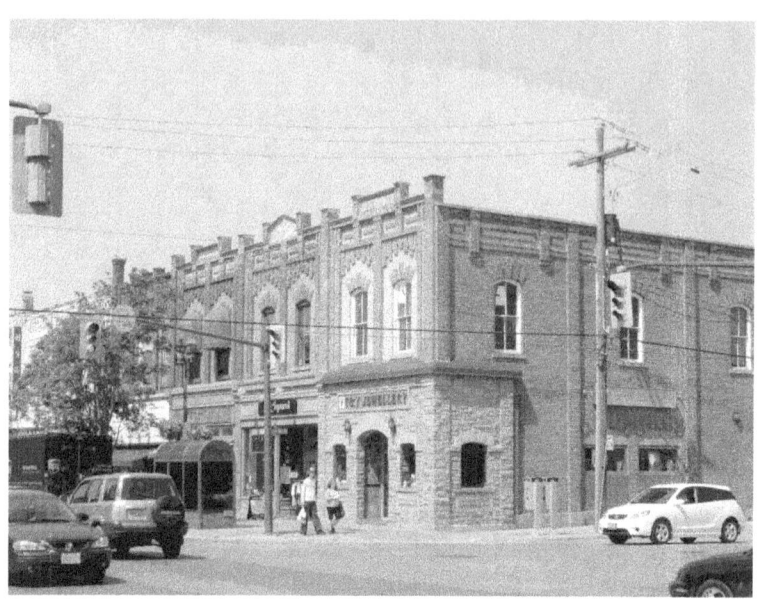

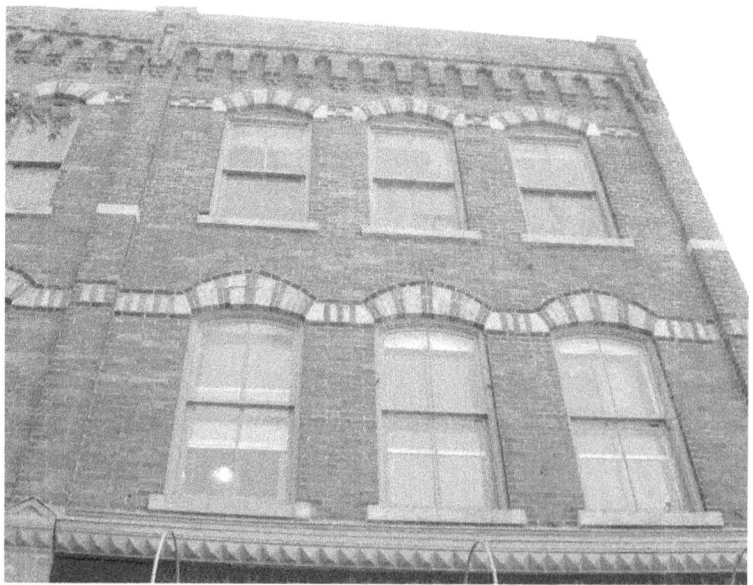
Dentil moulding, dichromatic window hoods

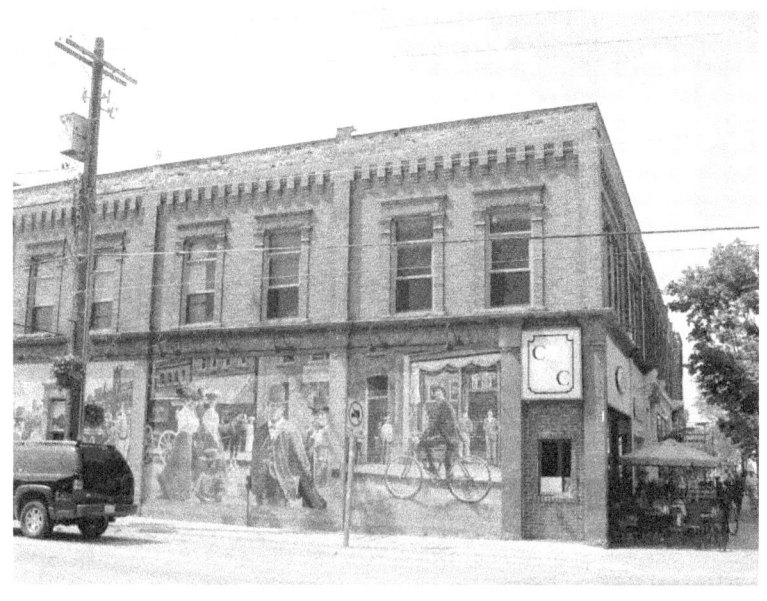

murals

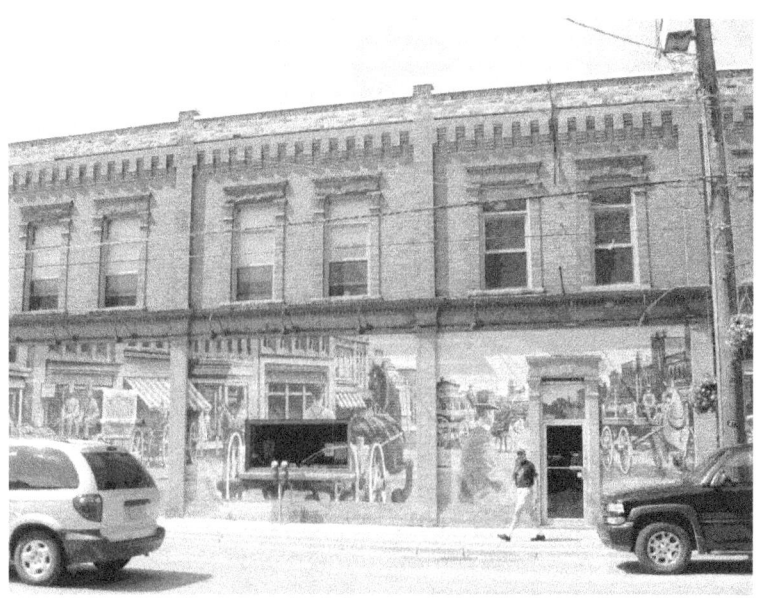

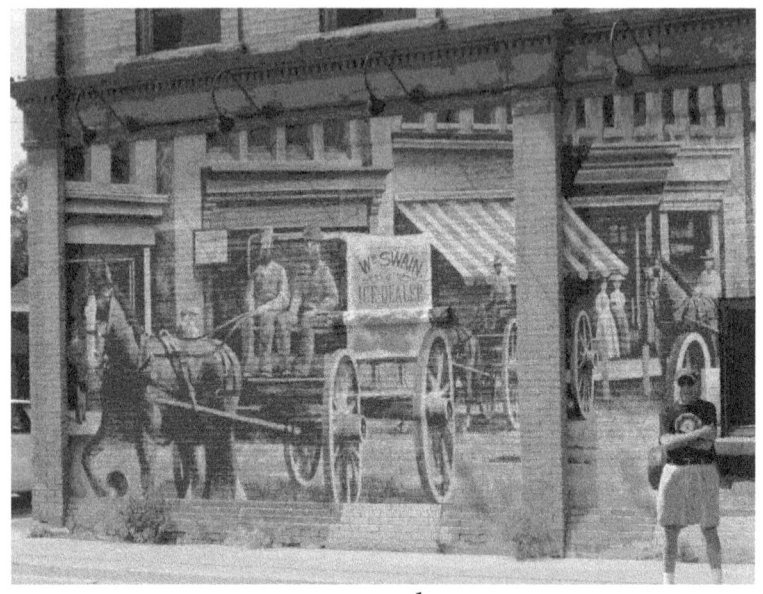
mural

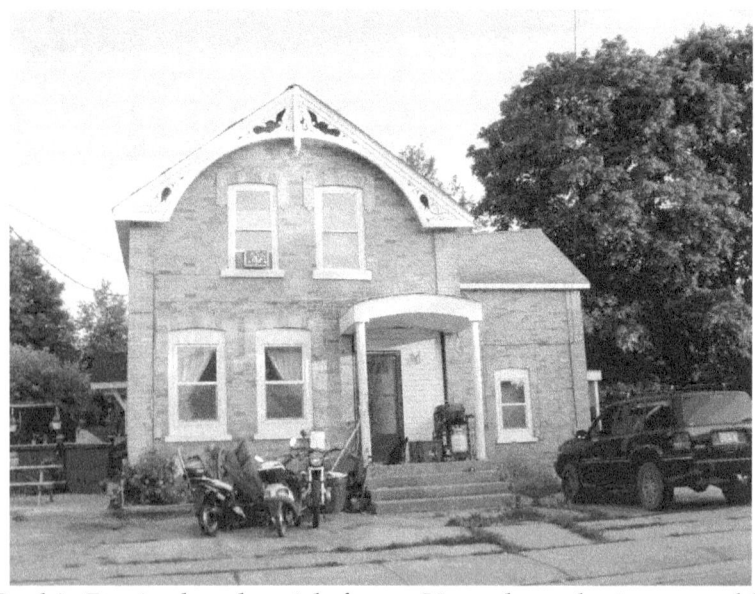
Gothic Revival style with fancy Vergeboard trim on gable

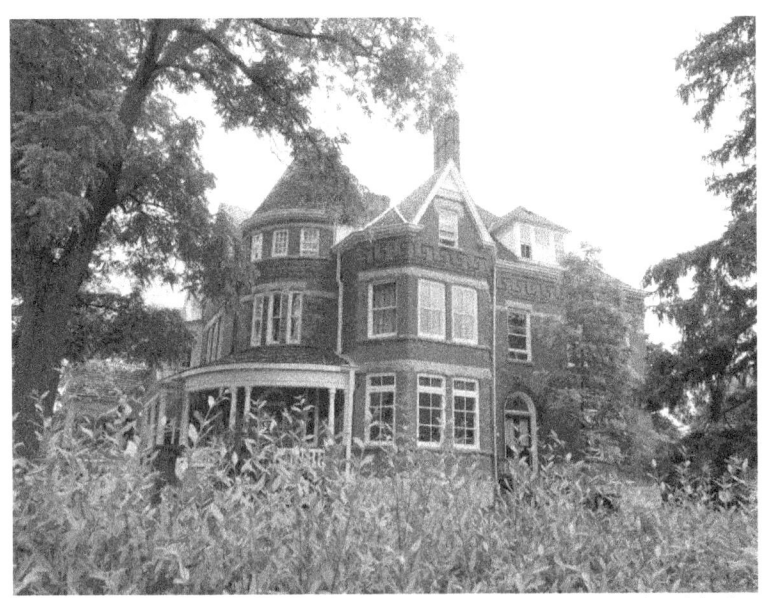

10,000 square foot home, "Tornaveen", three storey, double brick, multiple gables, a turret with conical roof, four tall ornamental chimneys, a large verandah with brick piers and turned columns, 80 windows of various sizes and styles – Queen Anne style. It now houses the National Ski Academy, 200 Oak Street

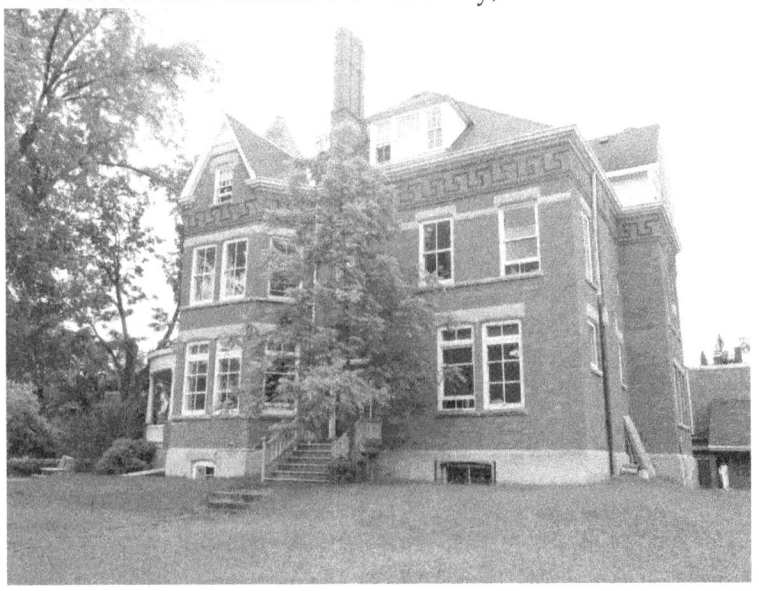

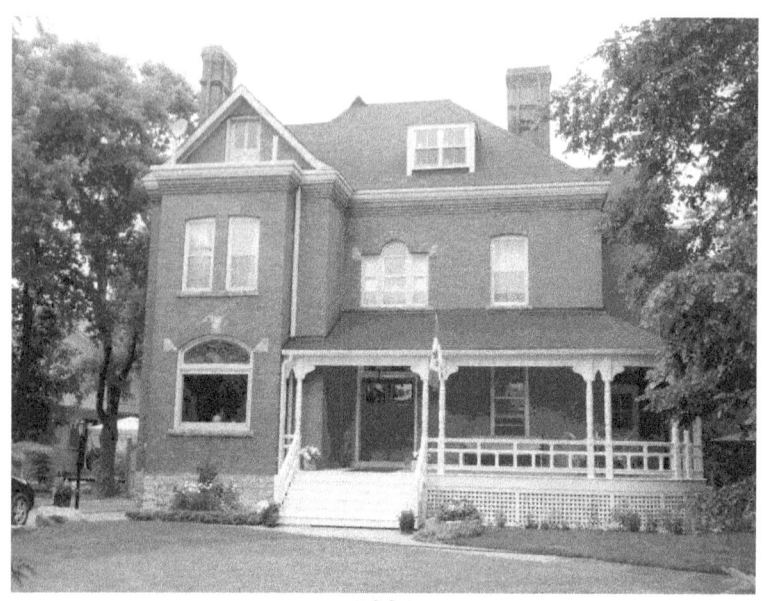

#291

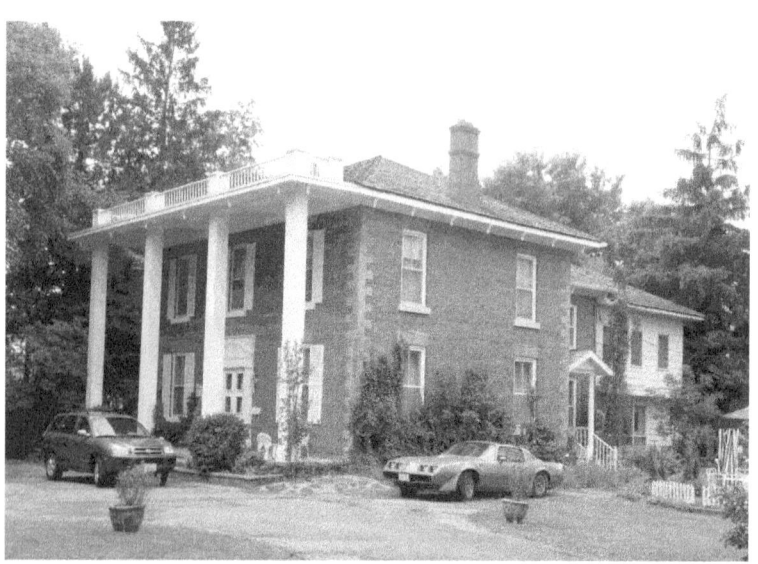

Struanhouse – R. Jacks - #329 – Italianate style

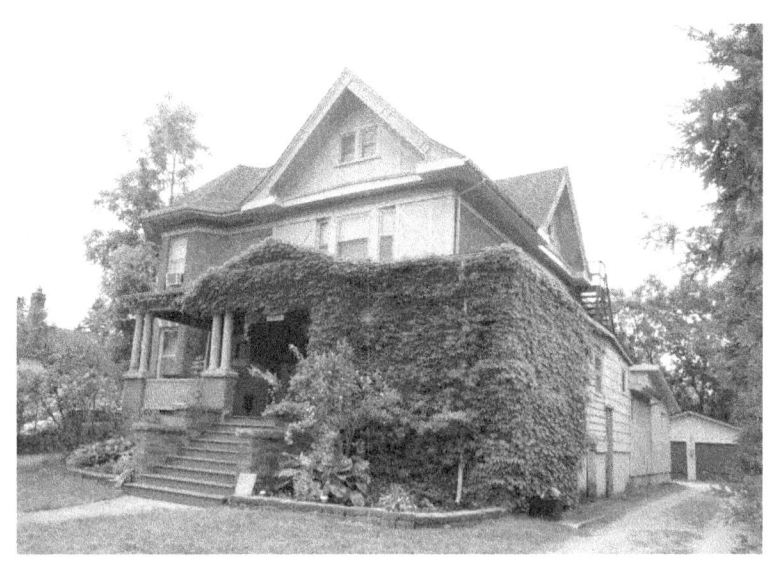

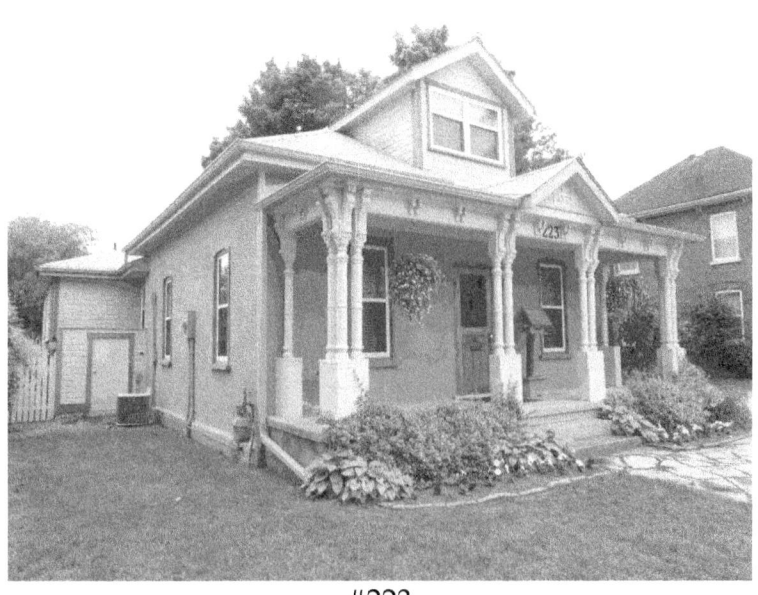

#223

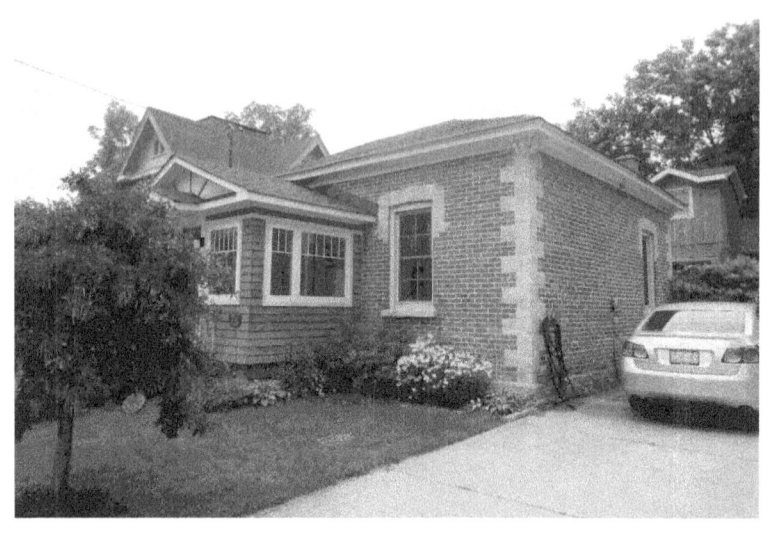

210 Cedar Street – Italianate style, dichromatic brickwork
Hip roof

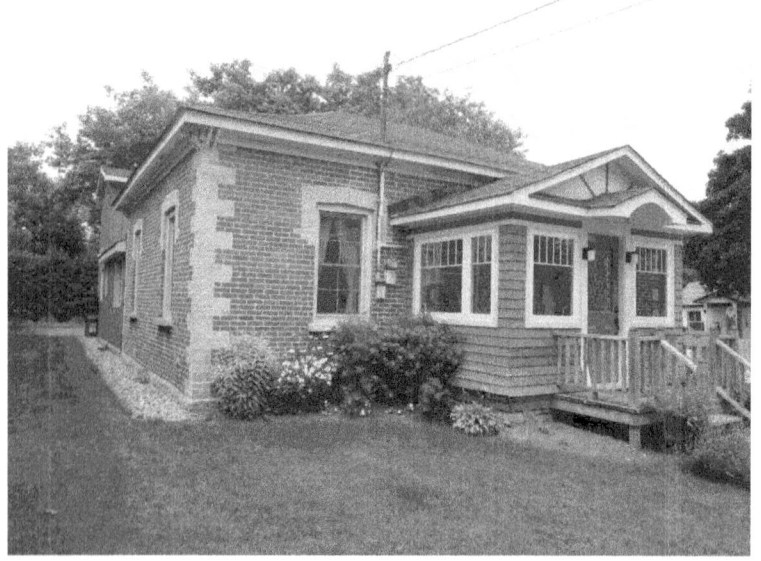

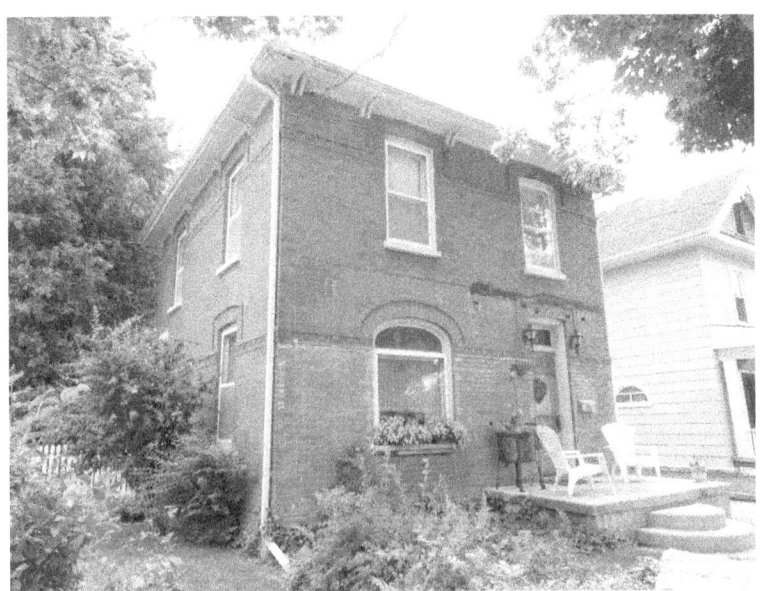

#233 – Italianate – paired cornice brackets

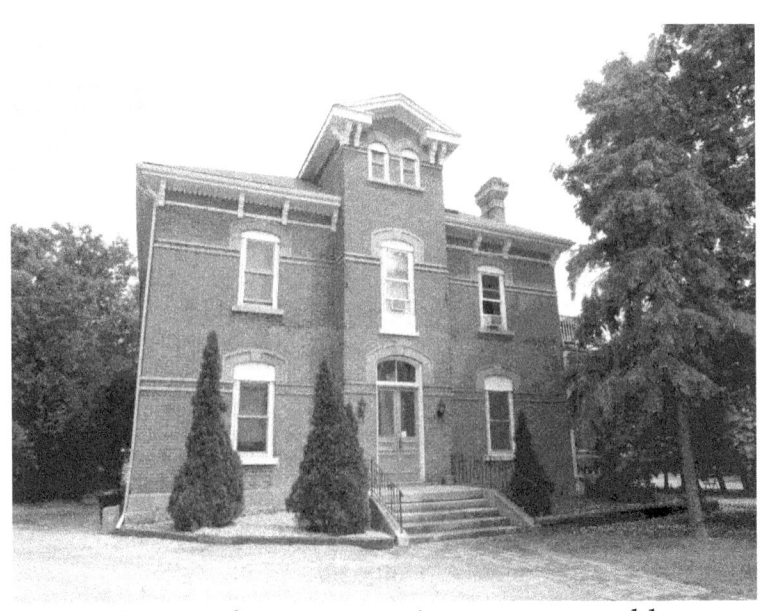

#217 – Italianate – cornice return on gable

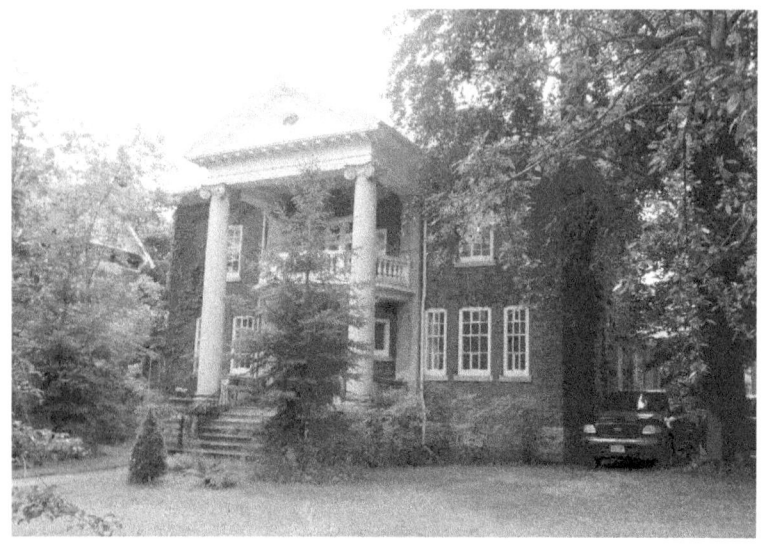

#242 – Italianate style – frontispiece with pediment and round pillars, circular balcony above front entrance

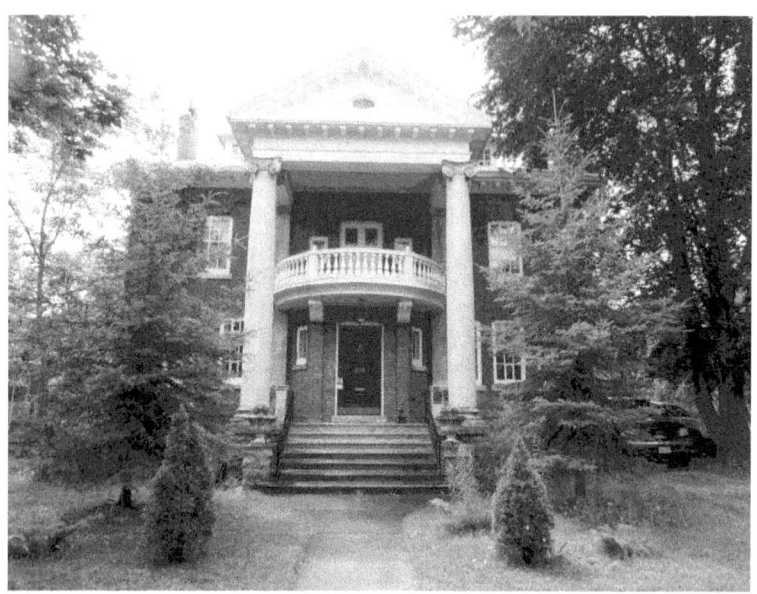

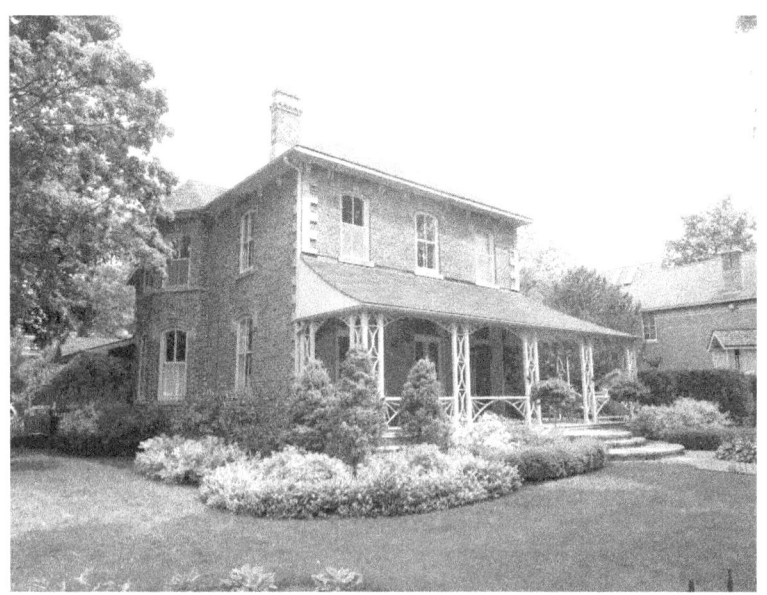

#199 – century home c. 1882 – Italianate – decorative chimney, quoining on corners, paired cornice brackets, keystones and voussoirs over windows

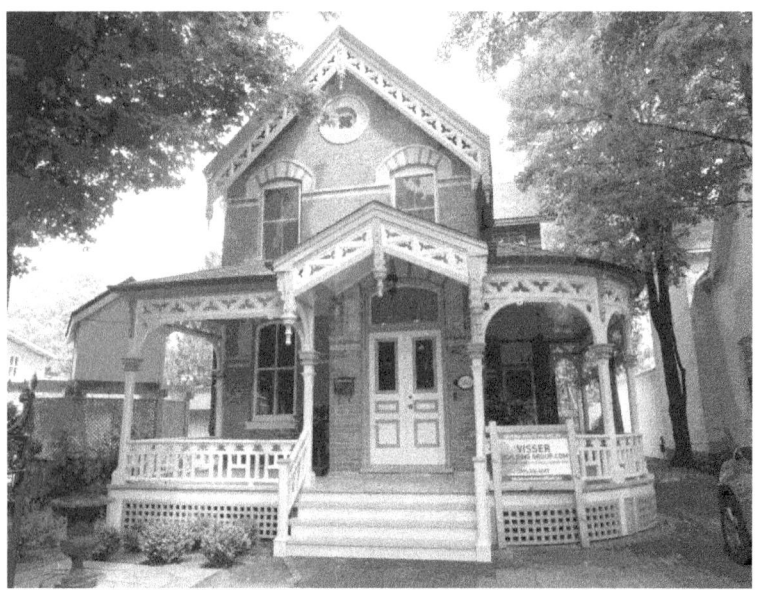

185 Third Street – elaborate Vergeboard trim – Gothic Revival style – dichromatic brickwork banding and window hoods

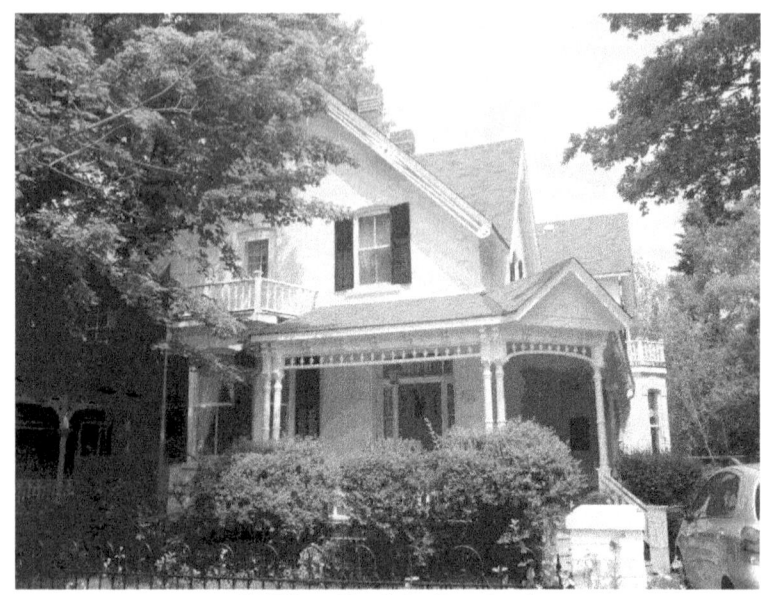

#175 – Gothic Revival

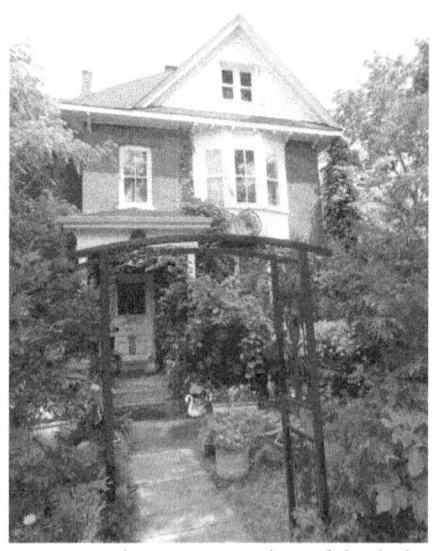

167 Third Street - Italianate with gabled dormer in attic

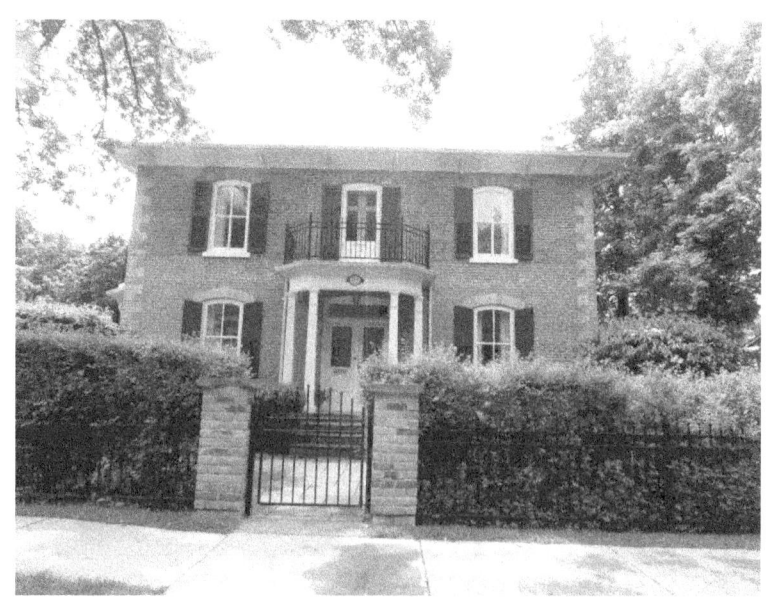

186 Third Street – Italianate style

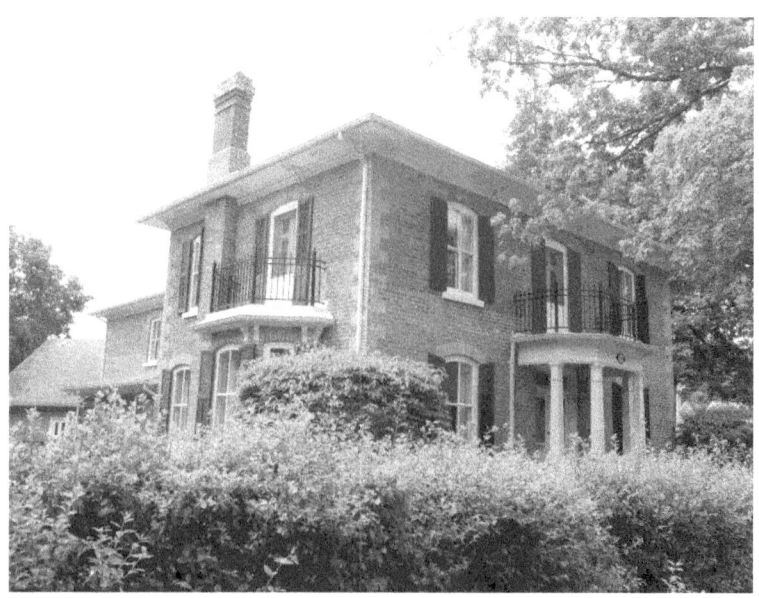

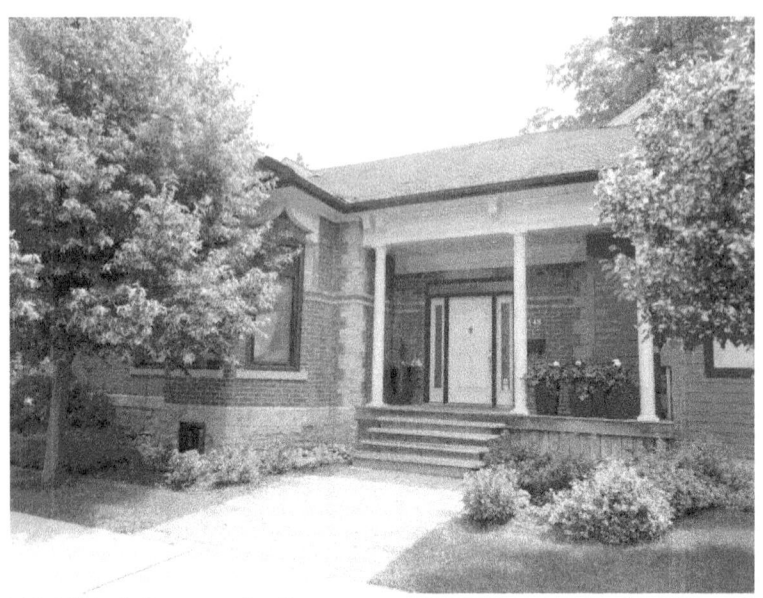

148 Third Street - Italianate with dichromatic brickwork

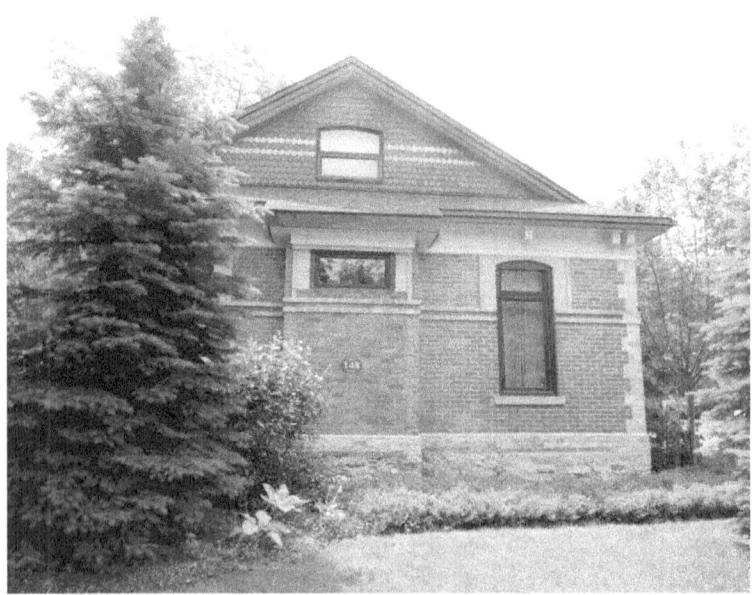

148 Third Street – Italianate with attic gable – quoining on corners, dichromatic brickwork, paired cornice brackets

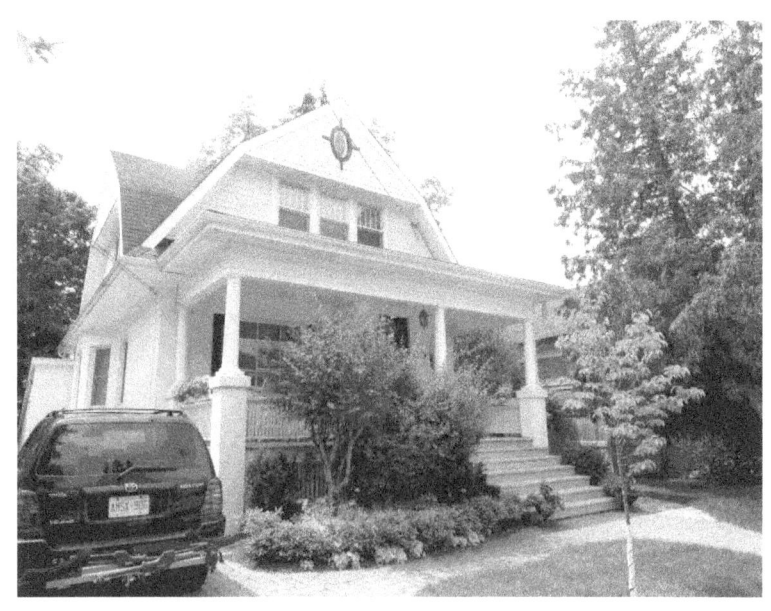

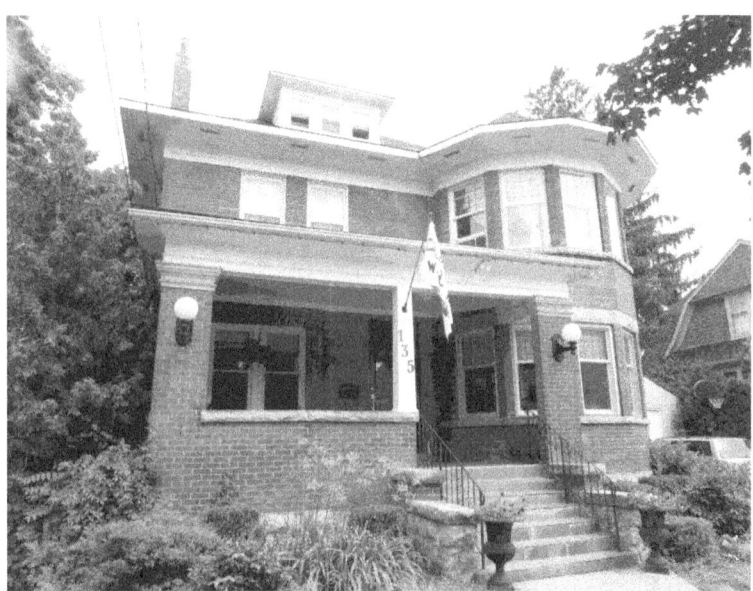

135 Third Street – two storey bay window, wide eaves, red brick, dormer out of roof

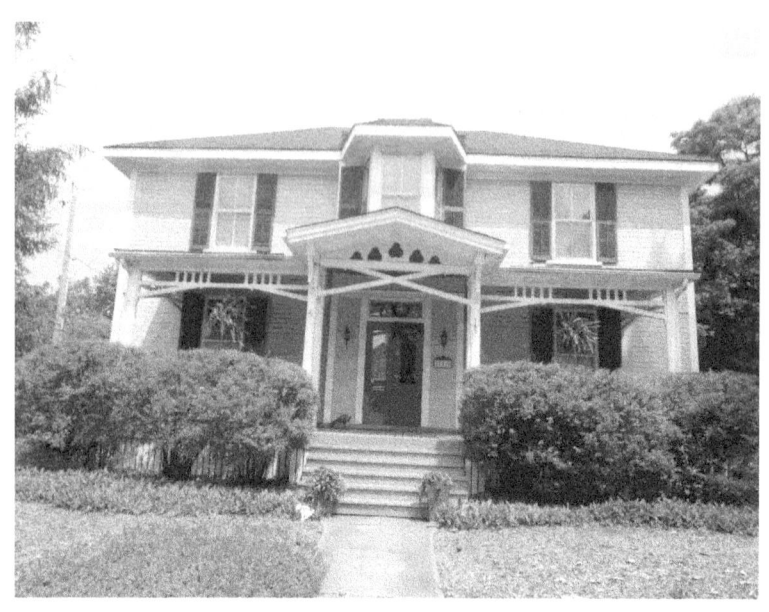

147 Third Street – Italianate with frontispiece
Upgraded with panelling

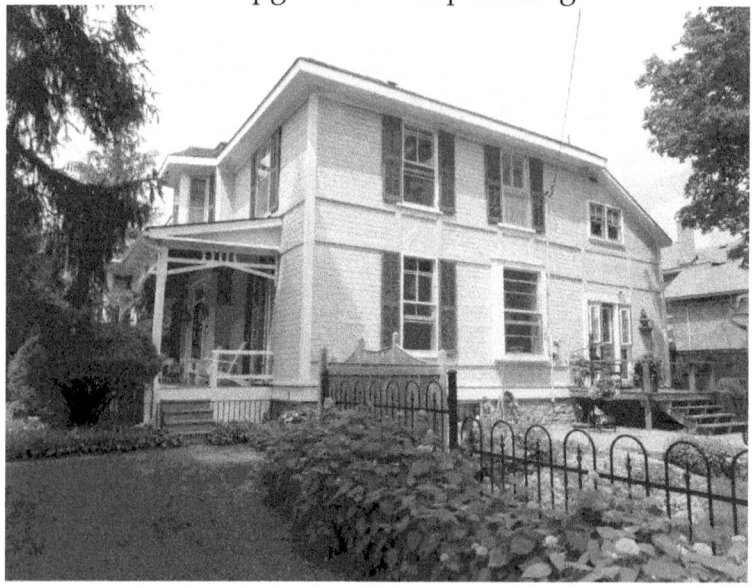

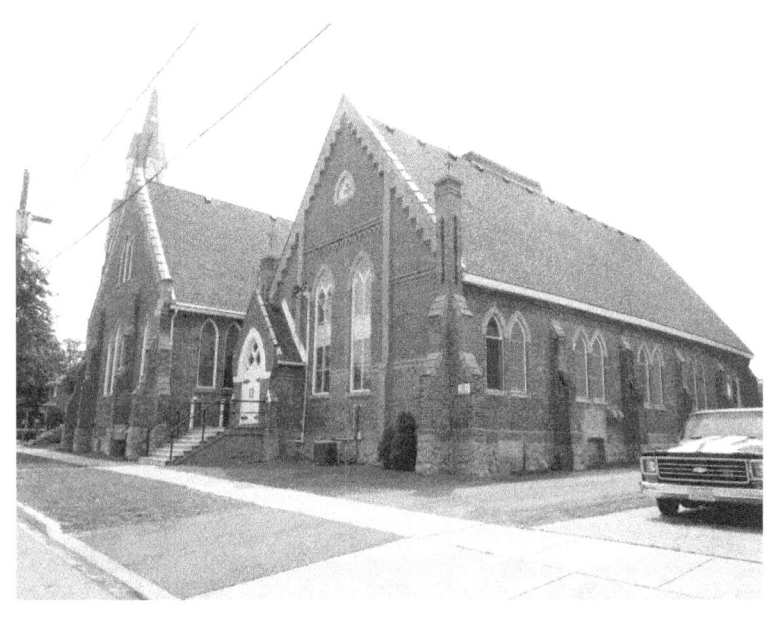

First Presbyterian Church, 200 Maple Street – erected 1884
Red brick, buttresses

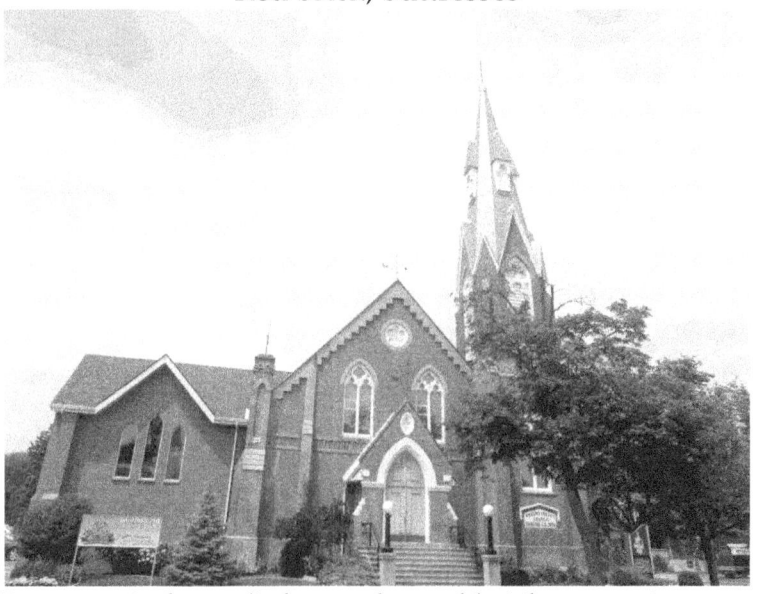

Lancet windows, lighter coloured brick voussoirs over windows

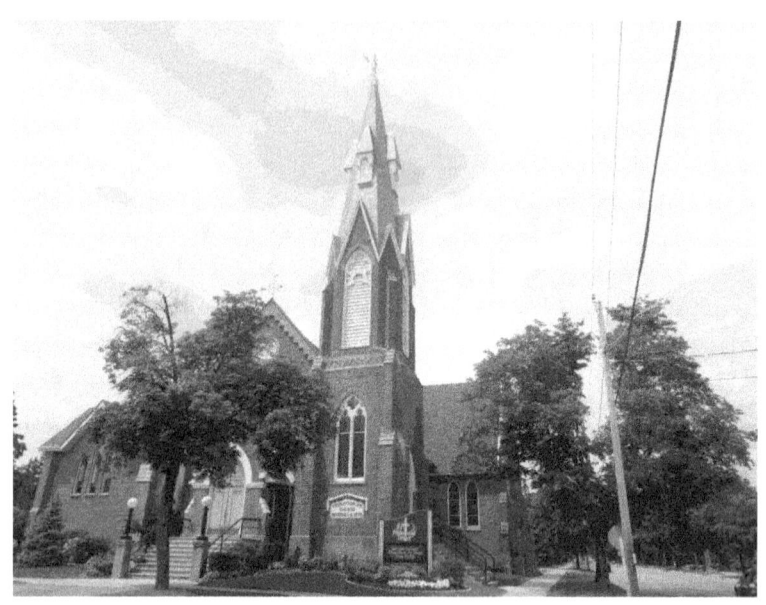

First Presbyterian Church – dichromatic brickwork

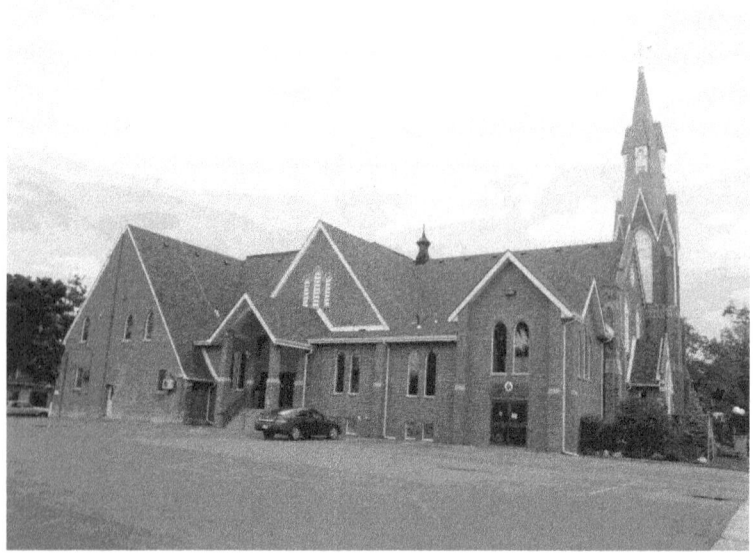

From rear

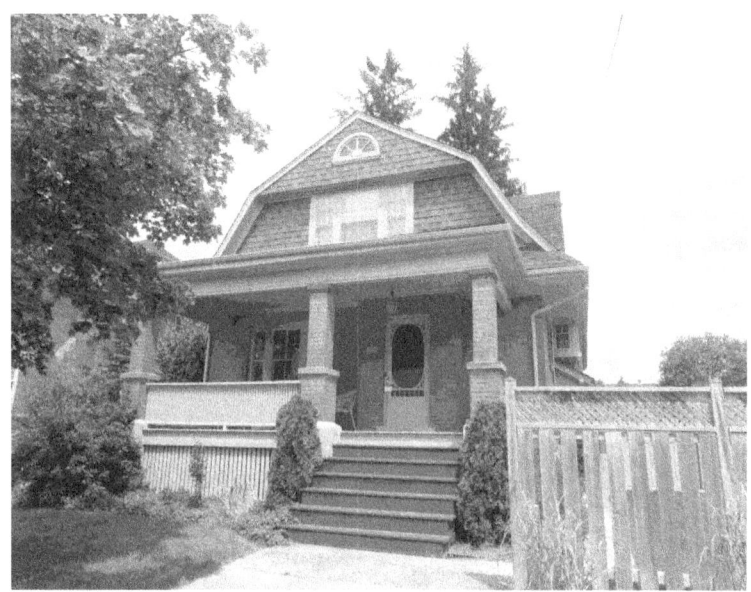

#125 - Edwardian style

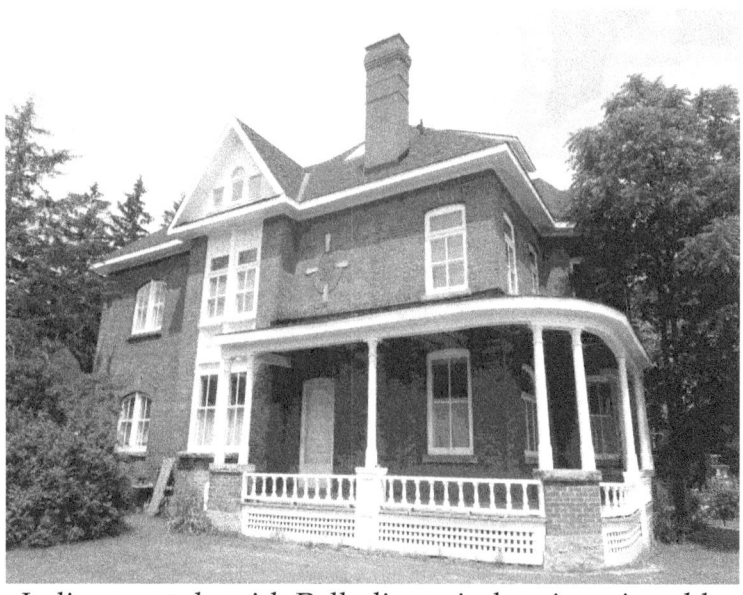

Italianate style with Palladian window in attic gable

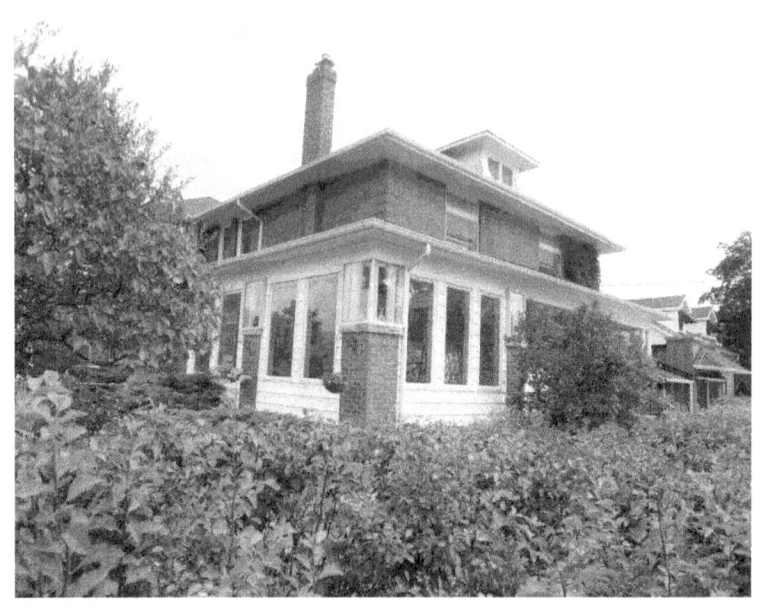

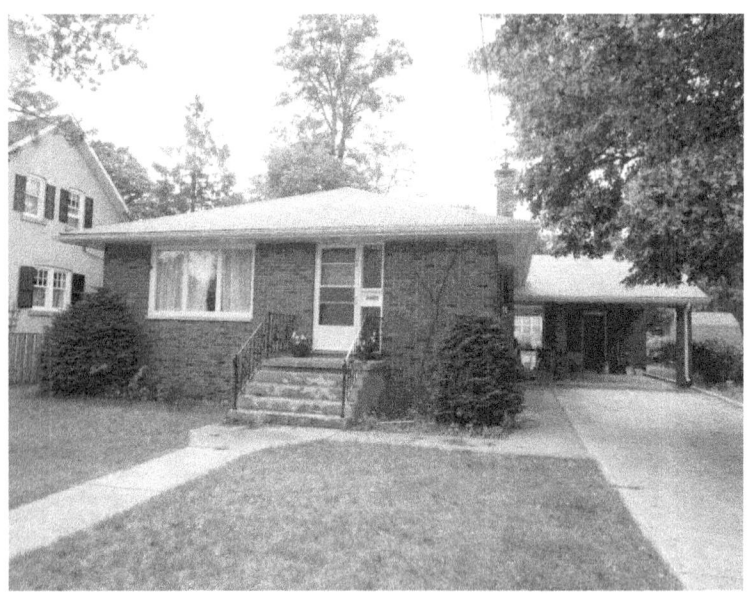

#88 - Regency Cottage

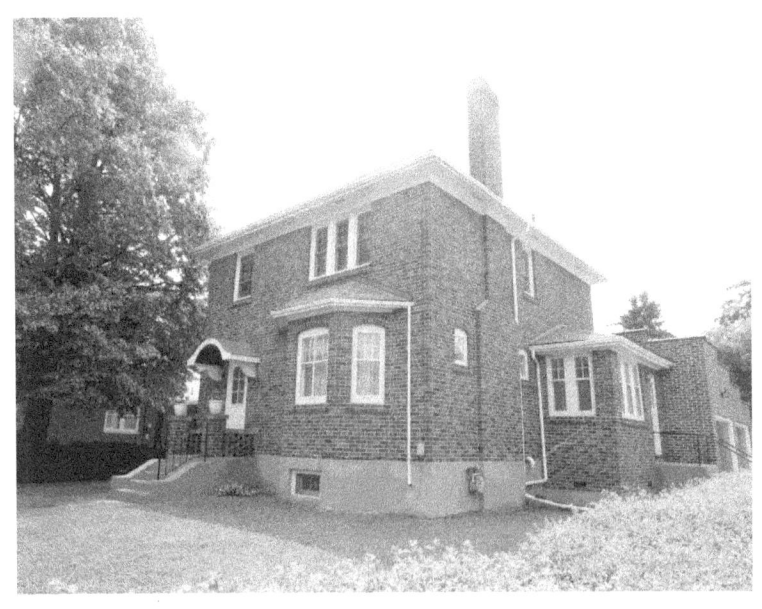

90 Third Street
Italianate with hipped roof, bay window, multi-coloured brick

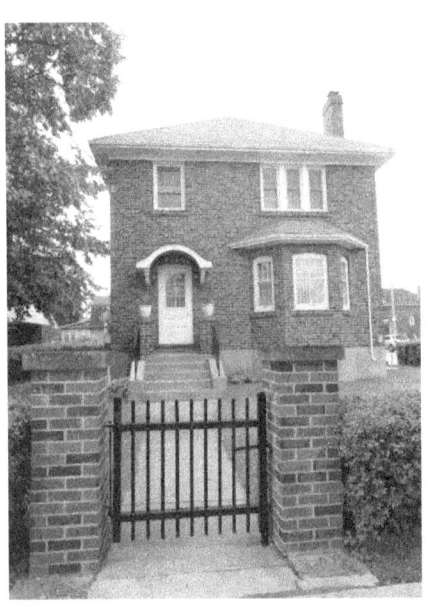

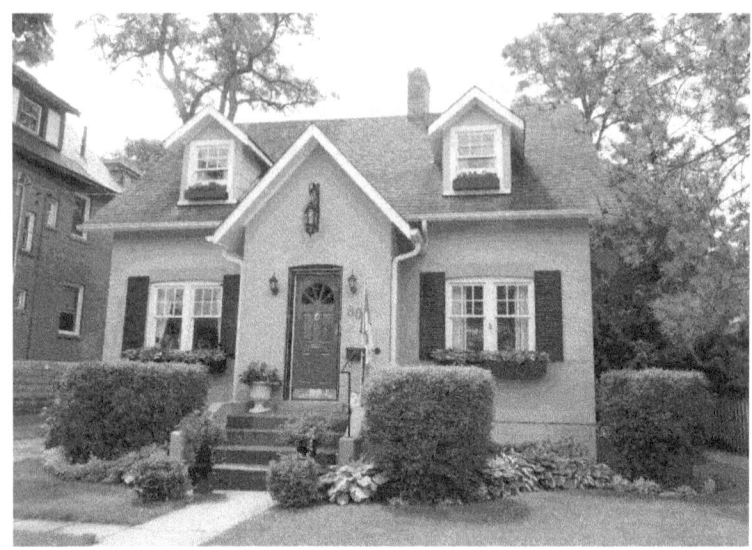

80 Third Street – Gothic Revival with dormer windows in attic

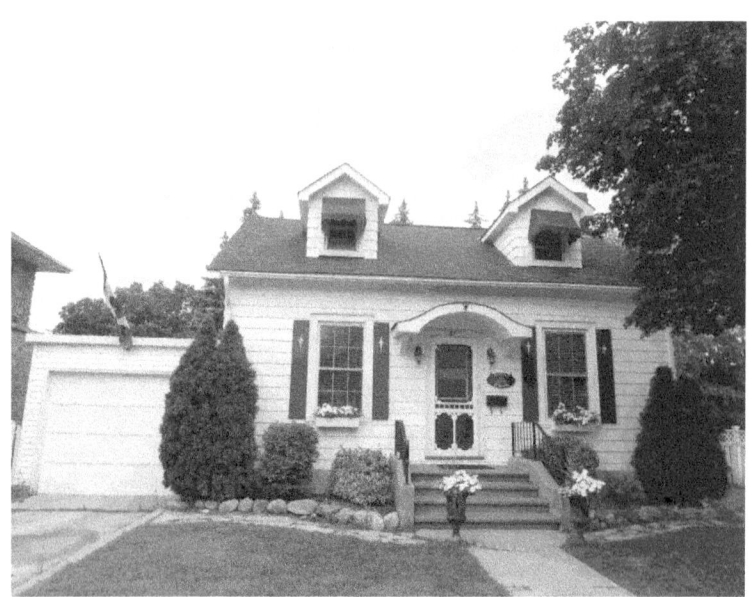

87 Third Street – Regency Cottage with dormers in attic

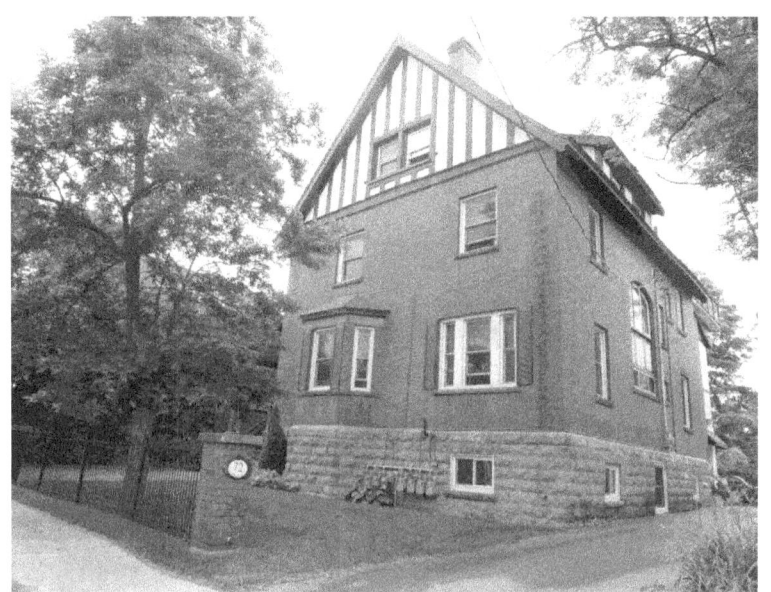

72 Third Street

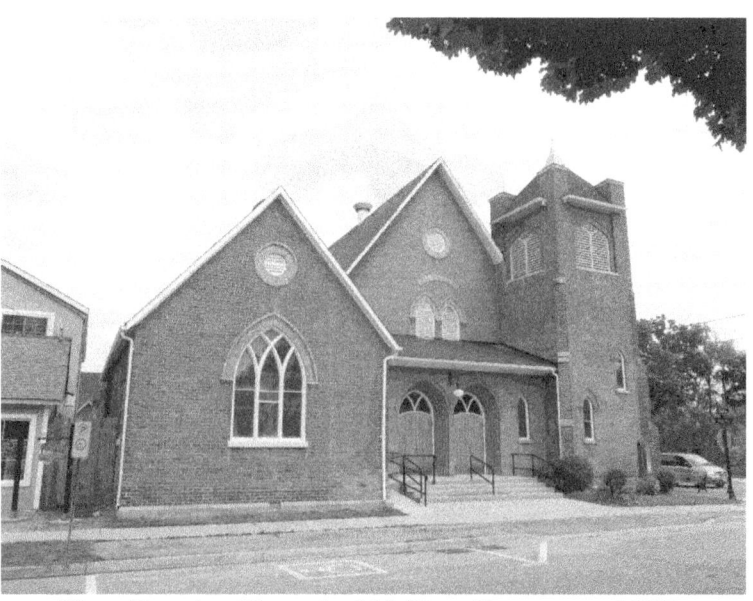

First Baptist Church, 160 Pine Street – c. 1870s
Gothic Revival style

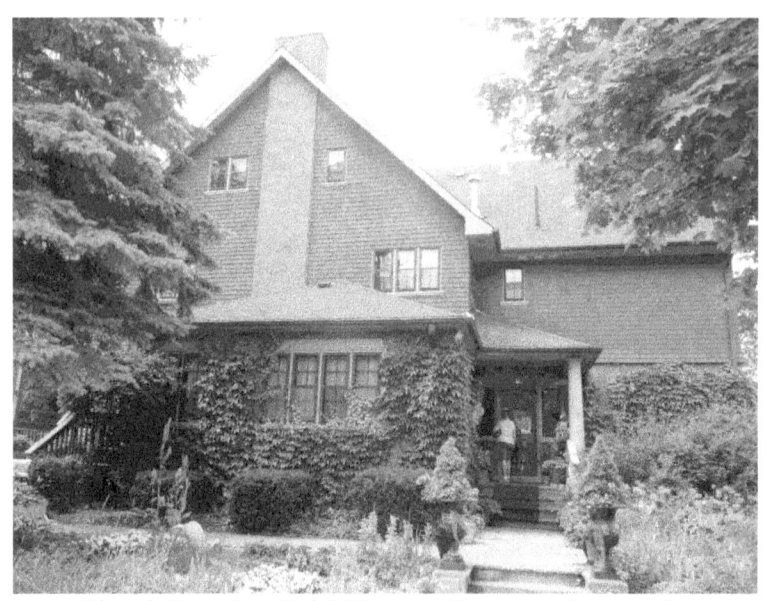
64 Third Street - Bield House Country Inn and Spa

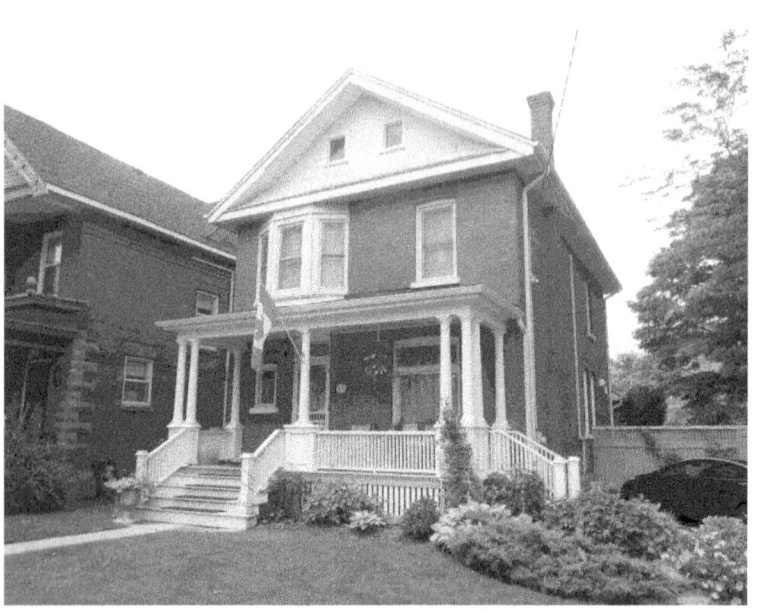
198 Pine Street - Edwardian style

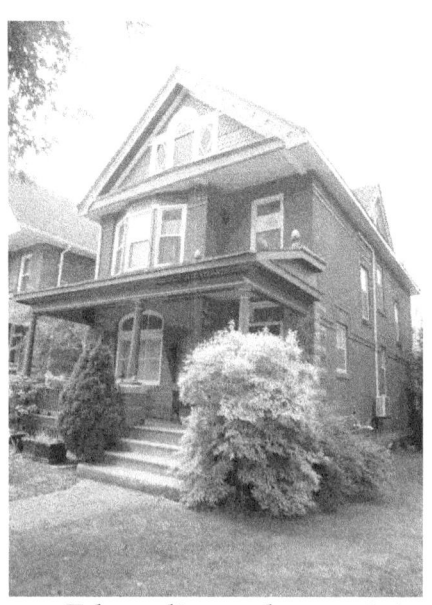

202 Pine Street – Edwardian style - quoining on corners, Palladian window in gable

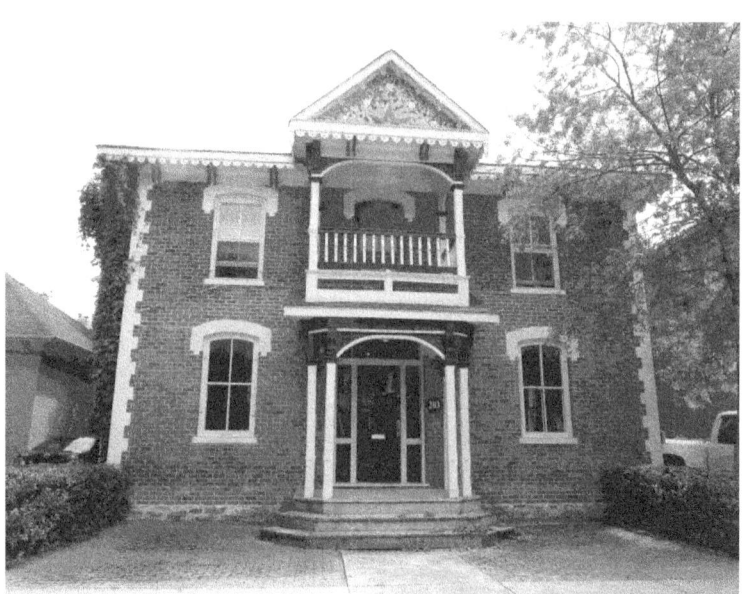

203 Pine Street – Italianate style – triangular pediment with decorated tympanum, lighter coloured window hoods, double cornice brackets, frontispiece supported by pillars

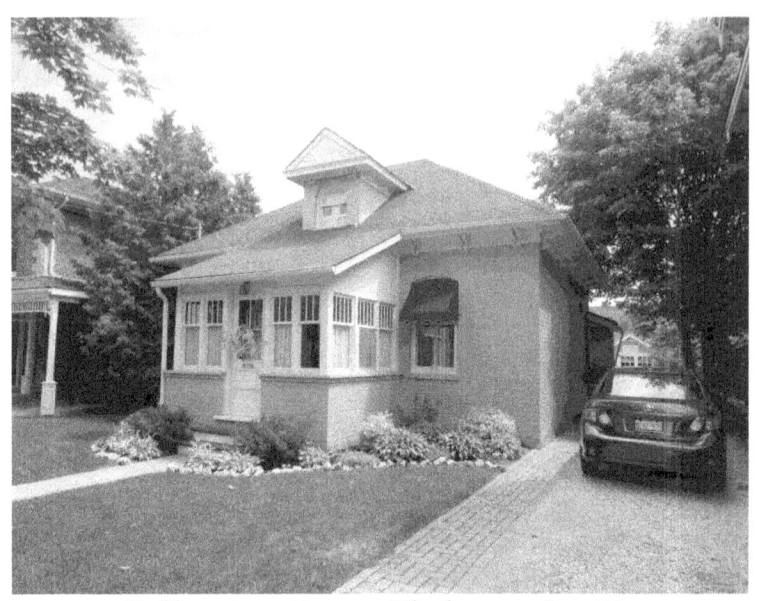
Italianate cottage with dormer in attic

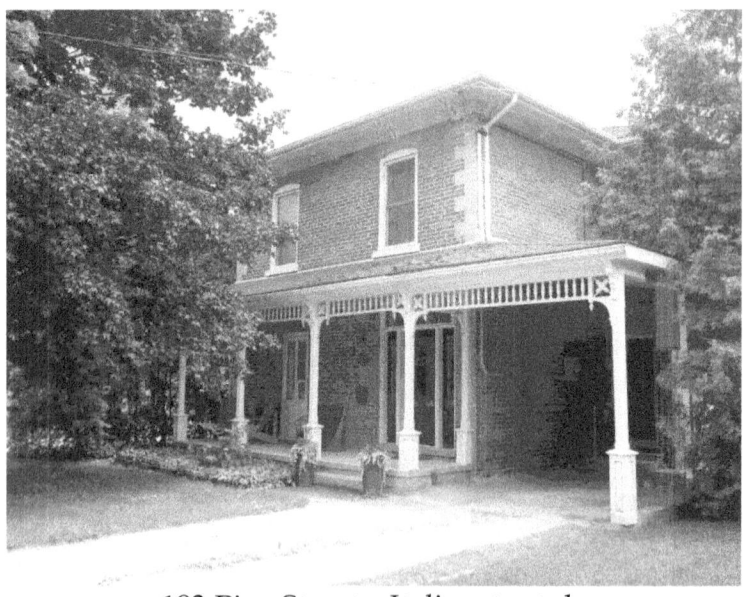
193 Pine Street – Italianate style

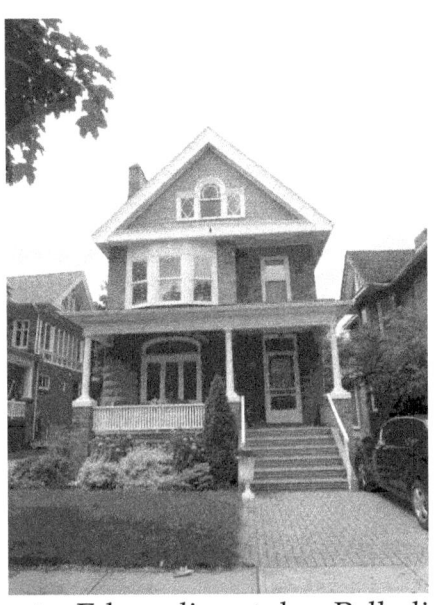

206 Pine Street – Edwardian style – Palladian window, bay window on second floor above verandah

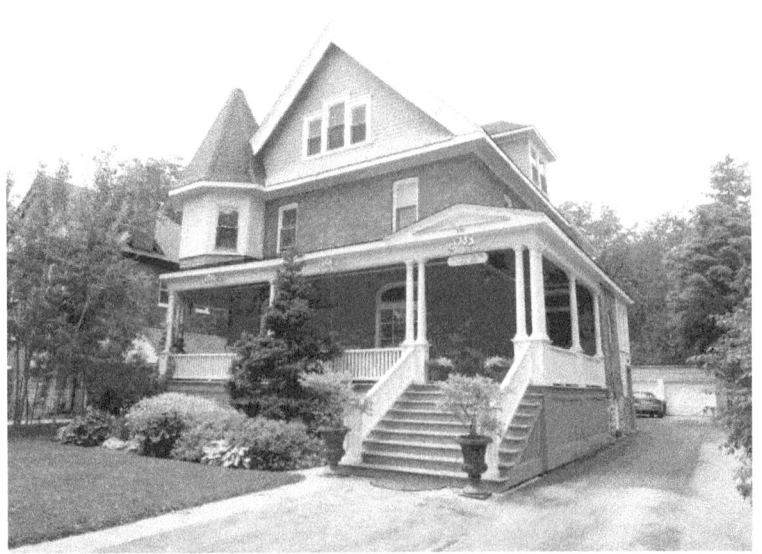

220 Pine Street – Edwardian style with Palladian window, and turret – c. 1910

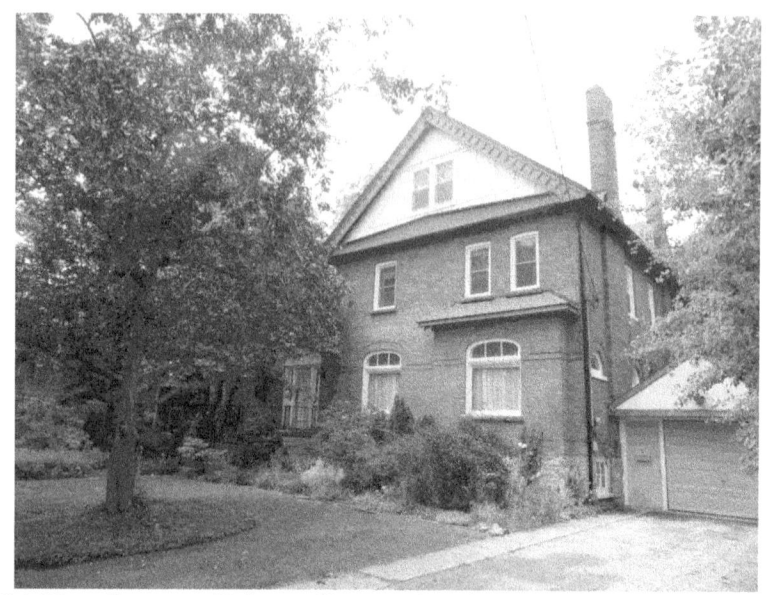

234 Pine Street – Edwardian style, decorative moulding on gable

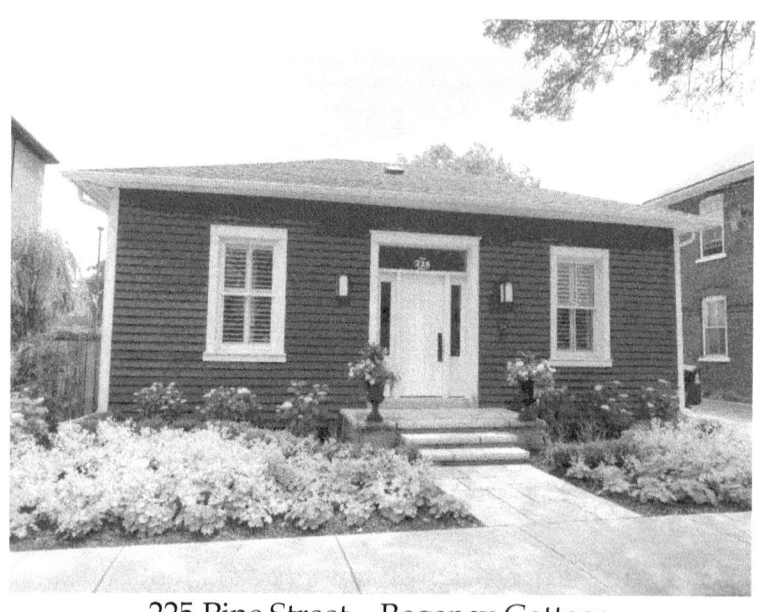

225 Pine Street – Regency Cottage

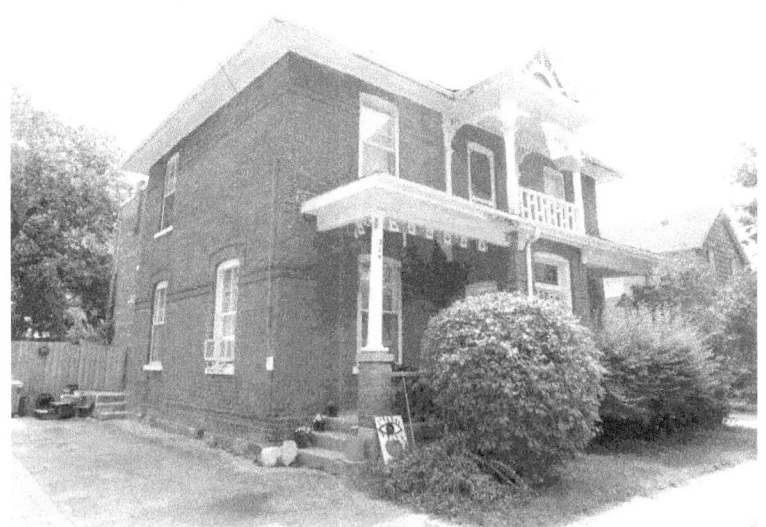

229 Pine Street - Italianate style with decorative frontispiece topped with triangular pediment and decorated tympanum

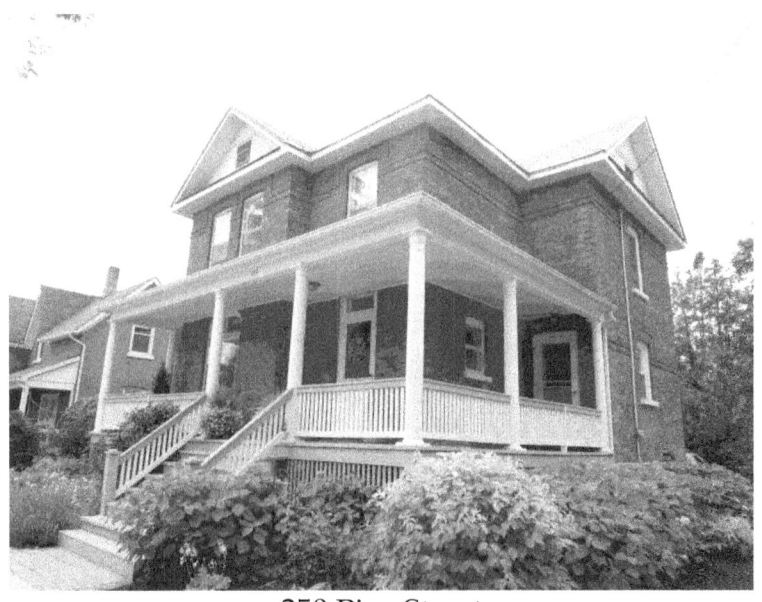

250 Pine Street

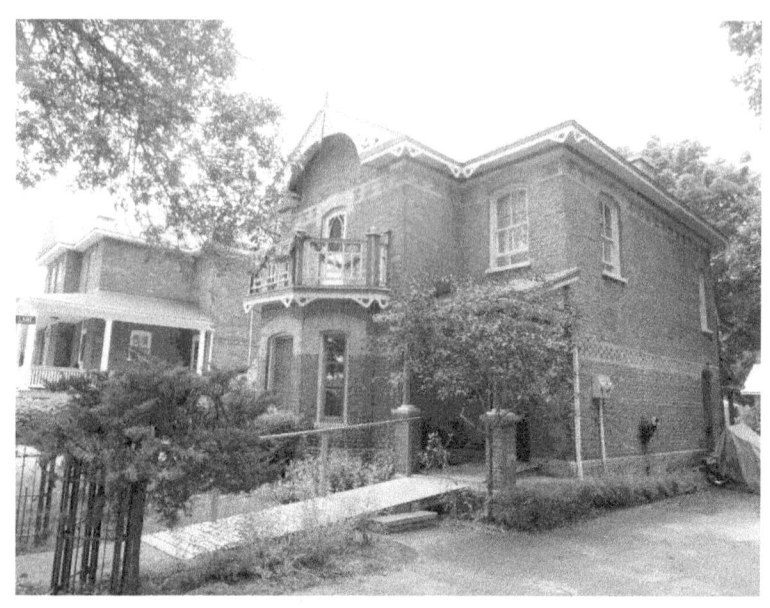

242 Pine Street - Italianate with Gothic style frontispiece, Vergeboard and finial, dichromatic brickwork

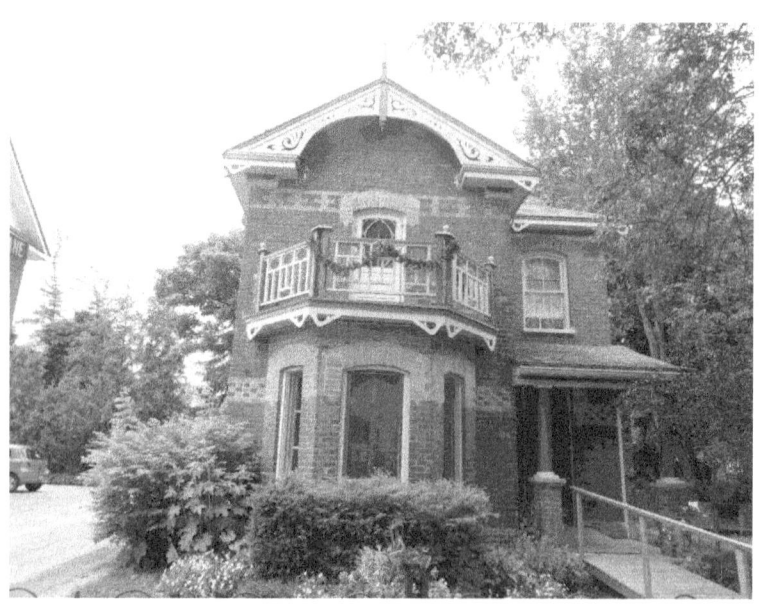

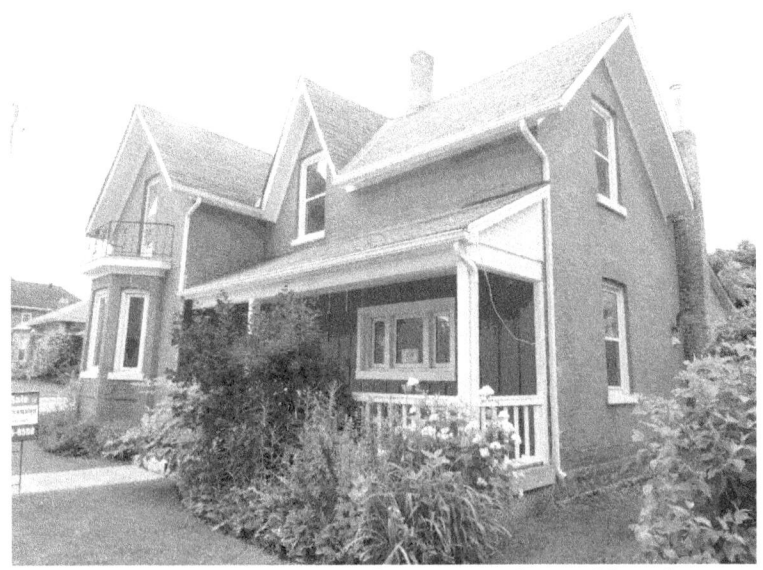

258 Pine Street – Gothic Revival – red brick

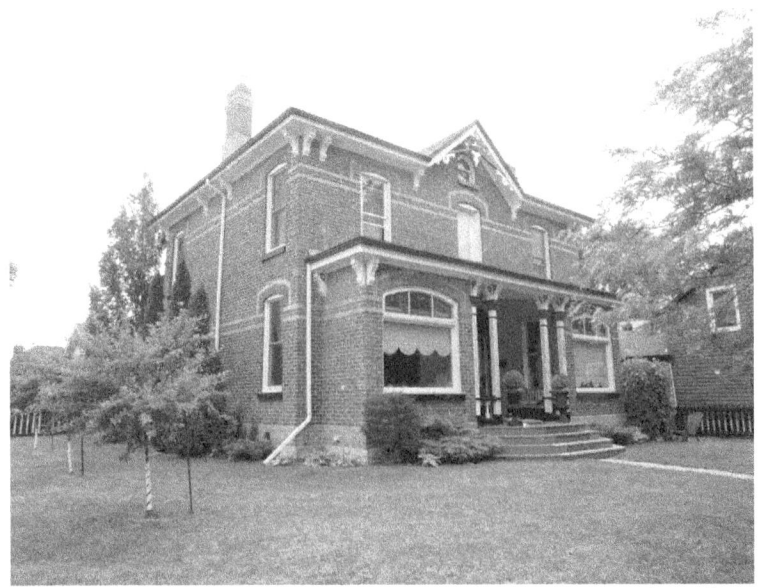

265 Pine Street – Italianate – decorative cornice brackets, Vergeboard trim on small gable, dichromatic brickwork

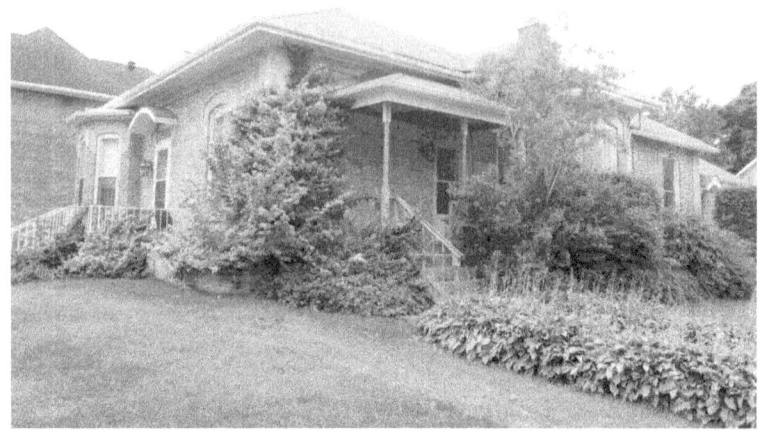

263 Pine Street - Regency Cottage

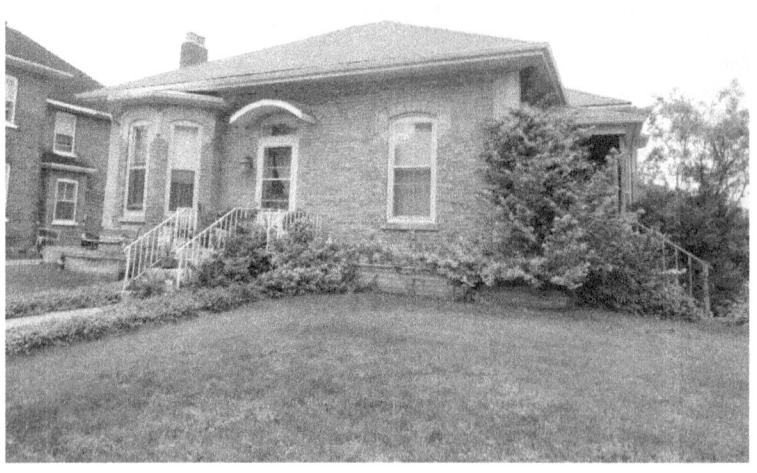

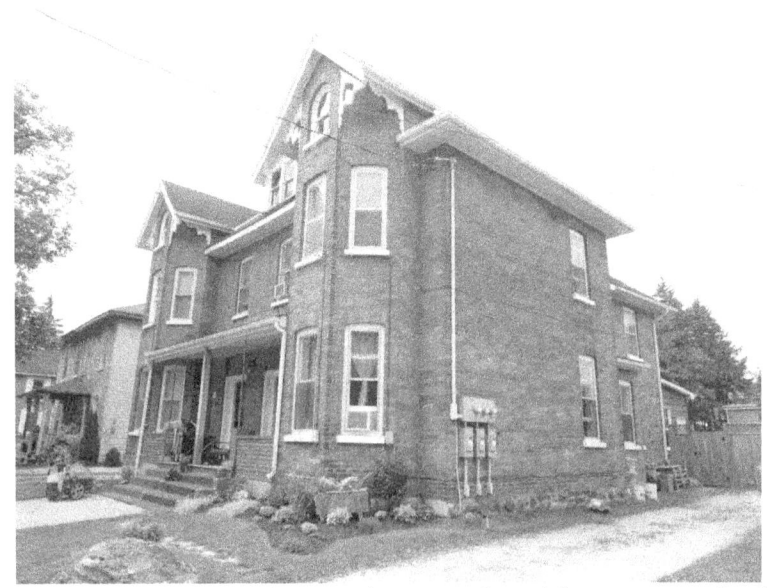

276, 278 Pine Street – Queen Anne style with a two-and-a-half storey tower-like bay with projecting eaves and large fretwork pieces resembling brackets. Cobblestone basement wall.

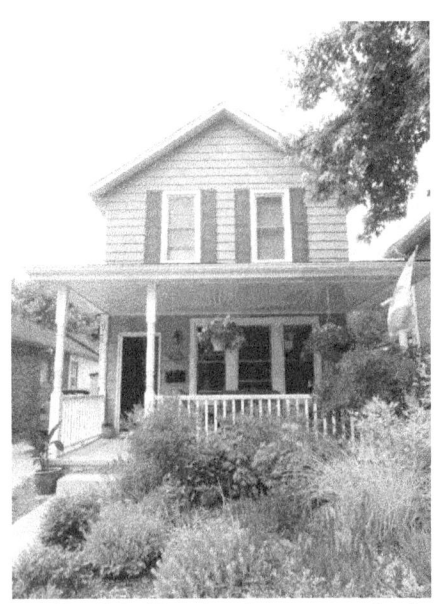

300 Pine Street – Gothic Revival – upgraded with panelling

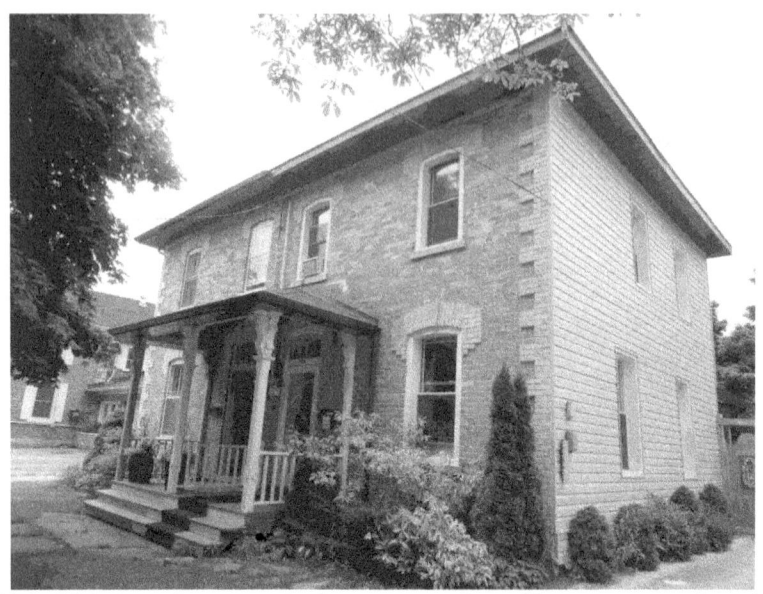

284, 286 Pine Street – Italianate style yellow-orange brick, quoin on corners, voussoirs above windows in buff coloured brick

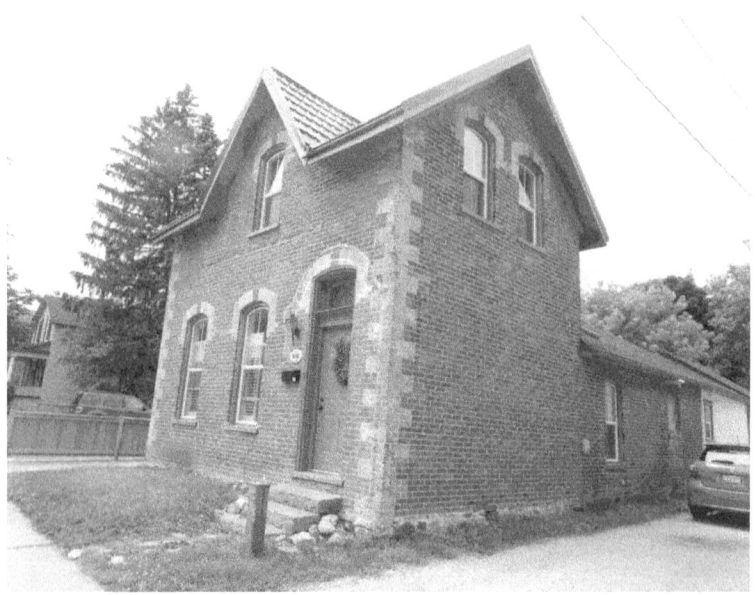

302 Pine Street - Gothic Revival with dichromatic quoining on corners, and buff coloured voussoirs

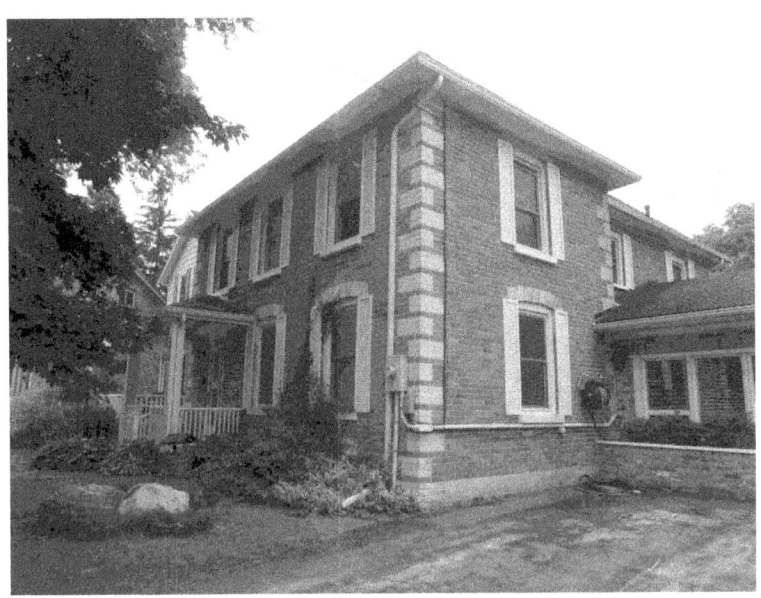

296 Pine Street – Italianate style – red brick with buff coloured accents

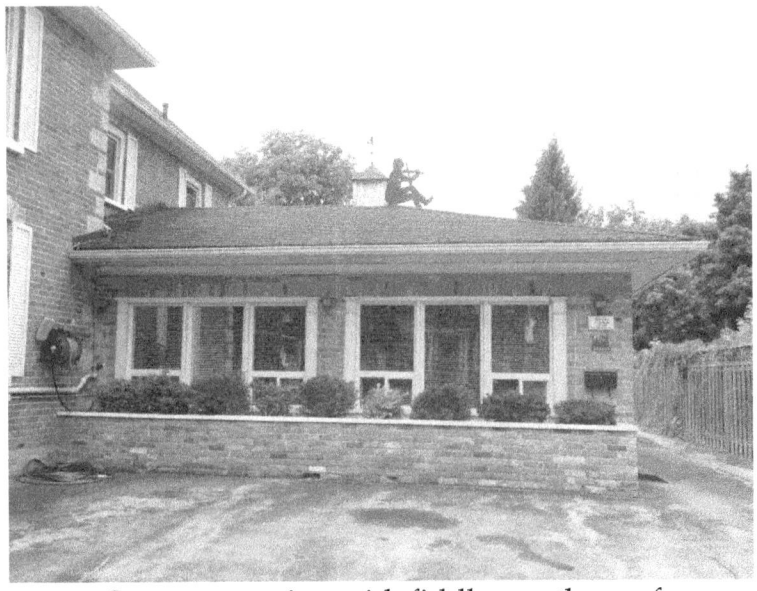

One storey wing with fiddler on the roof
The first date Harry and I went on was to see "Fiddler on the Roof"

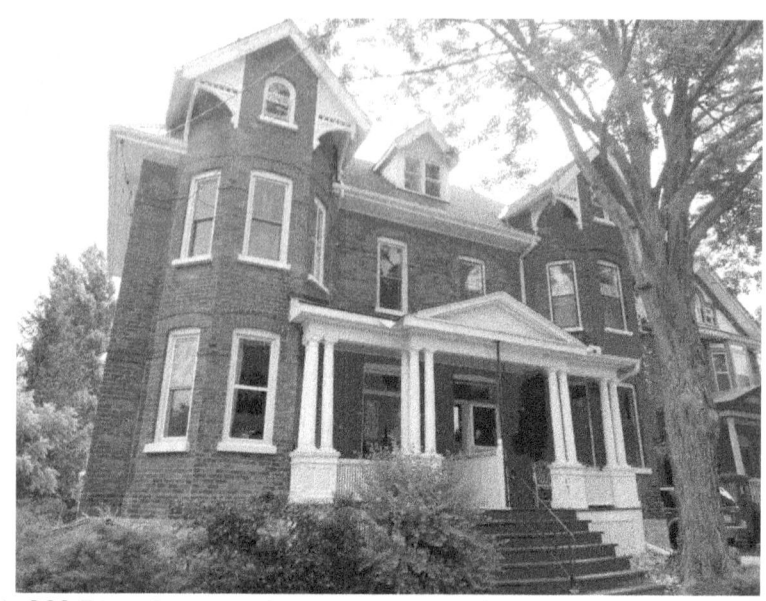

291, 293 Pine Street – Queen Anne style with a two-and-a-half storey tower-like bay with projecting eaves and large fretwork pieces resembling brackets.

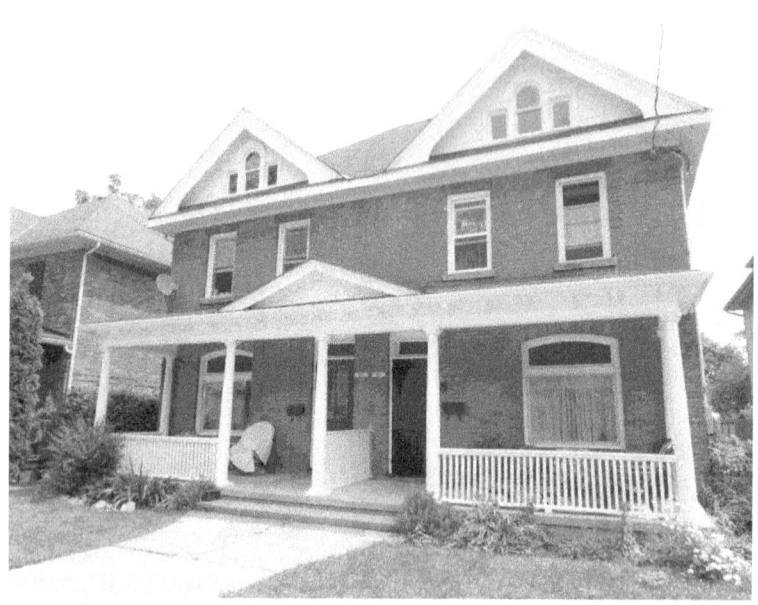

311, 313 Pine Street – Edwardian style with Palladian windows in gables

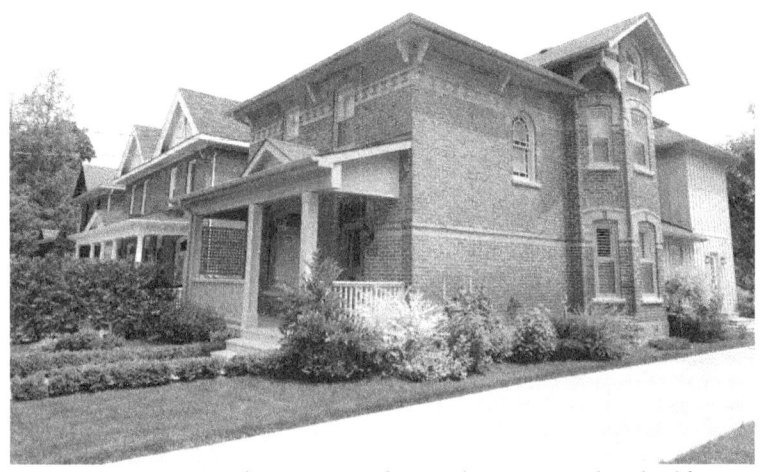

317 Pine Street - Italianate style with two-and-a-half-storey bay with projecting eaves and large fretwork pieces resembling brackets.

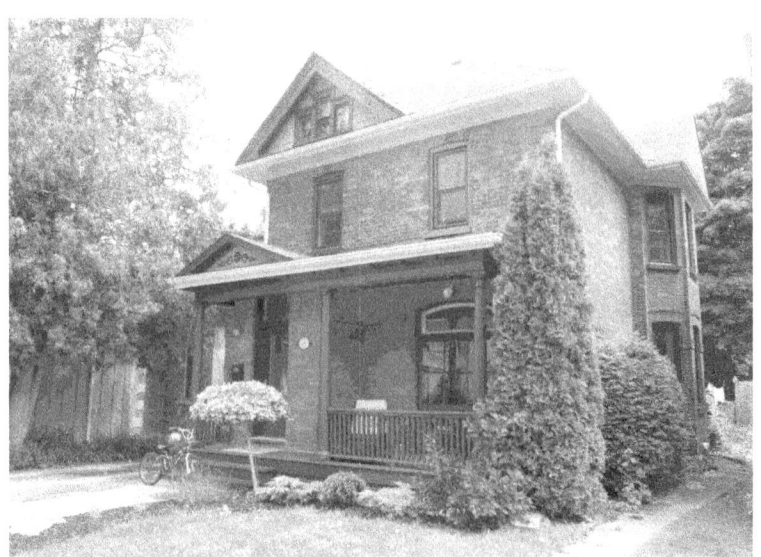

305 Maple Street – Edwardian/Italianate style – Palladian window, triangular pediment with decorated tympanum

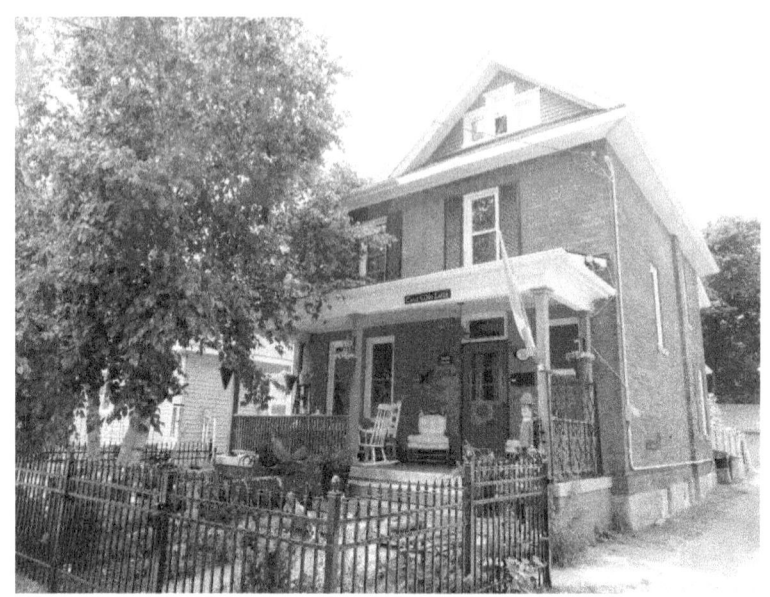

312 Maple Street – Maple Manor – Edwardian – Palladian window

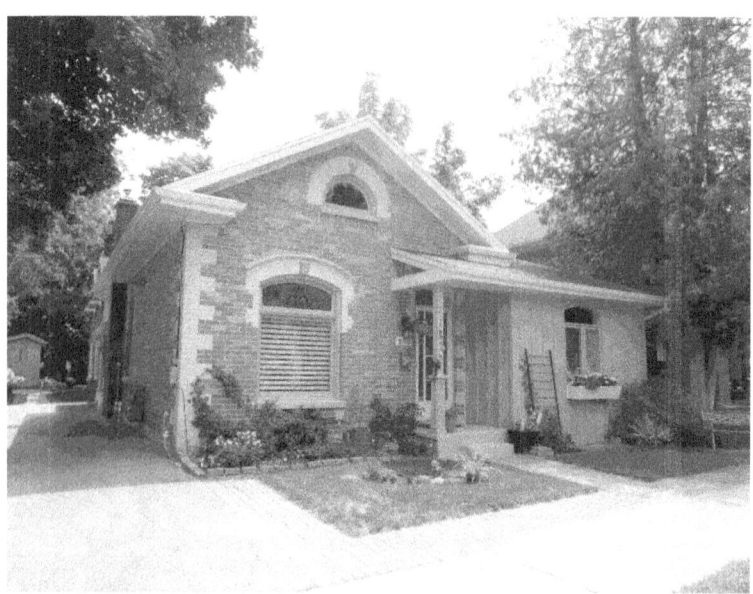

299 Maple Street – 1½ storey Gothic cottage with dichromatic brickwork, buff coloured voussoirs, keystones colour of walls, cornice return on gable ends

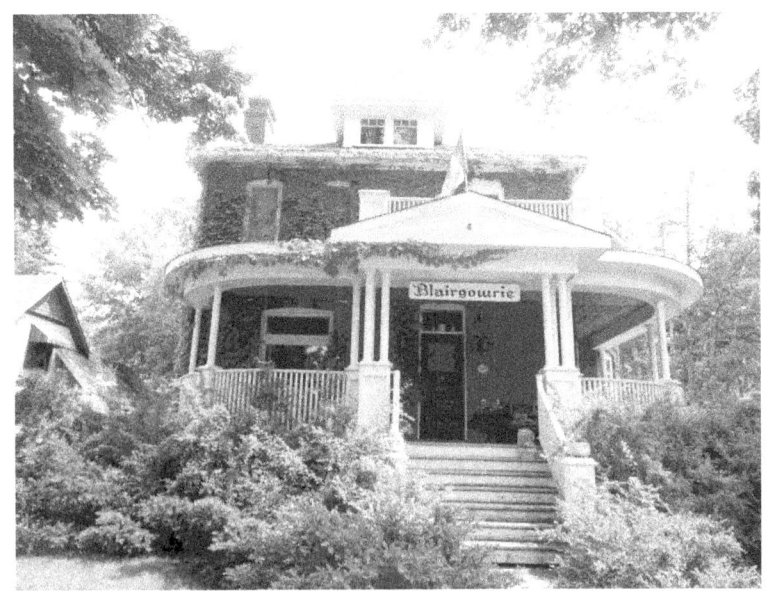

291 Maple Street – Blairgowrie – Italianate – wrap-around verandah, triangular pediment supported by pillars

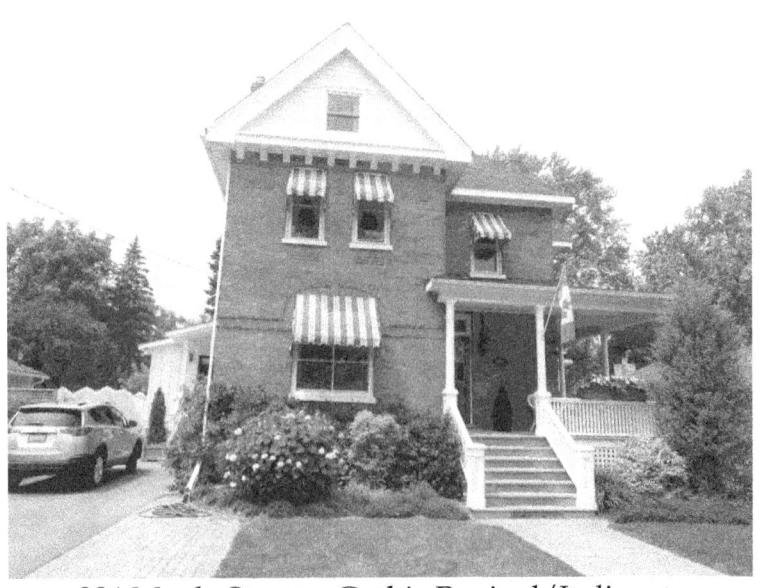

284 Maple Street – Gothic Revival/Italianate

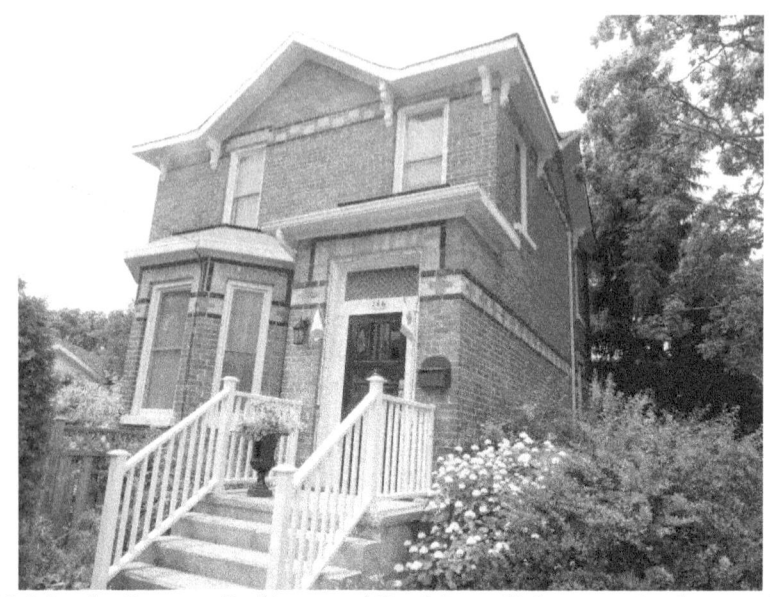

266 Maple Street - Italianate/Gothic – dichromatic decorative brickwork, bay window, single cornice brackets

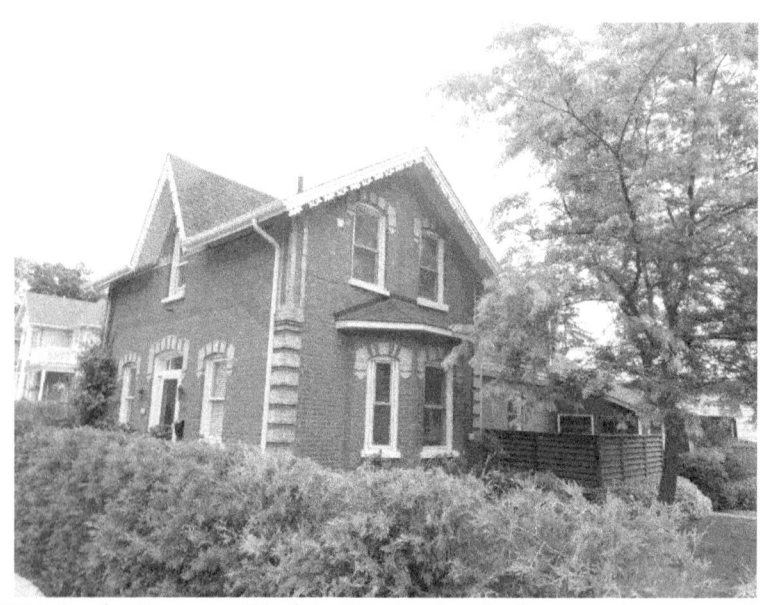

255 Maple Street – Gothic Revival – dichromatic voussoirs, Vergeboard on gables, corner quoins

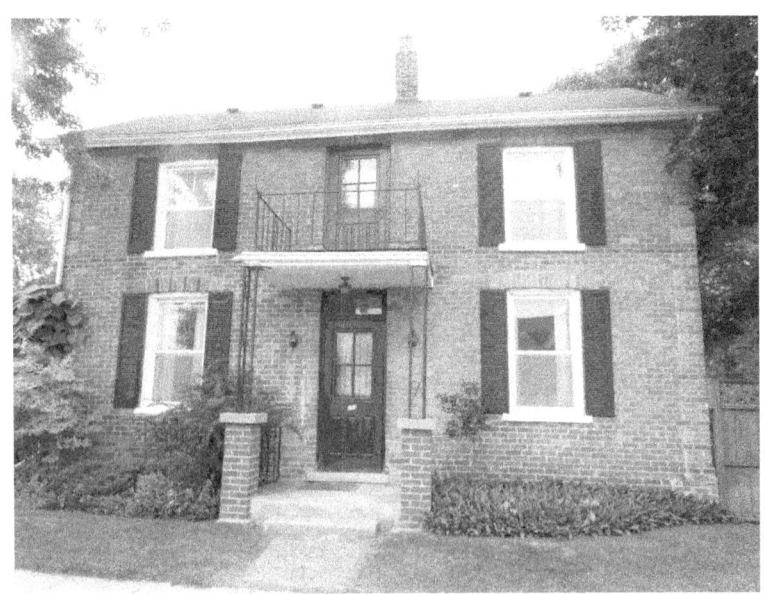

258 Maple Street - Georgian style

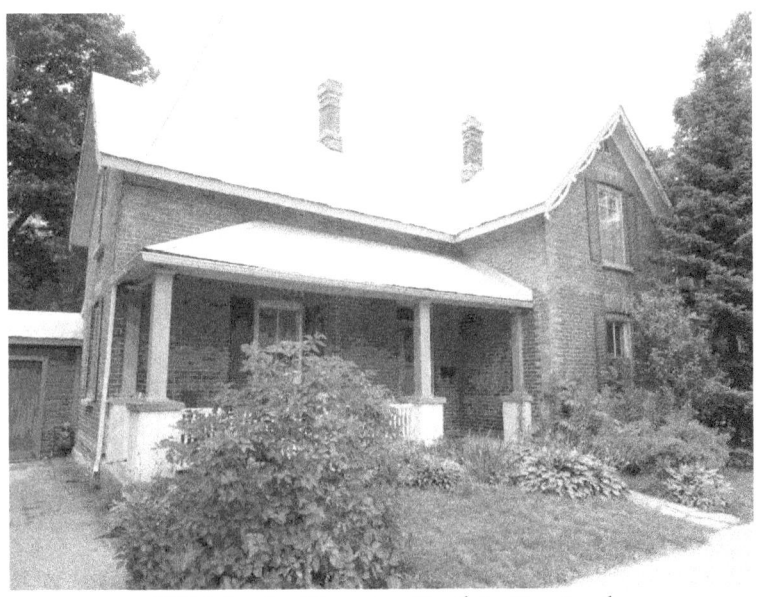

250 Maple Street – Gothic Revival

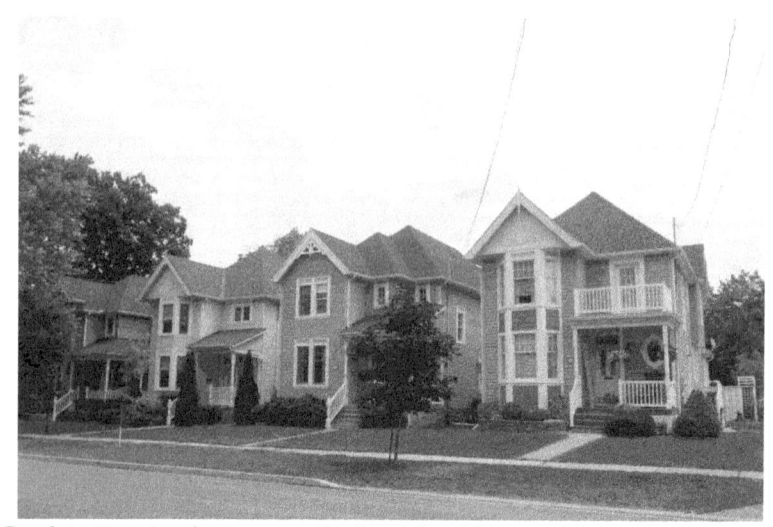

Gothic Revival – upgraded with siding – Vergeboard and finial on gables

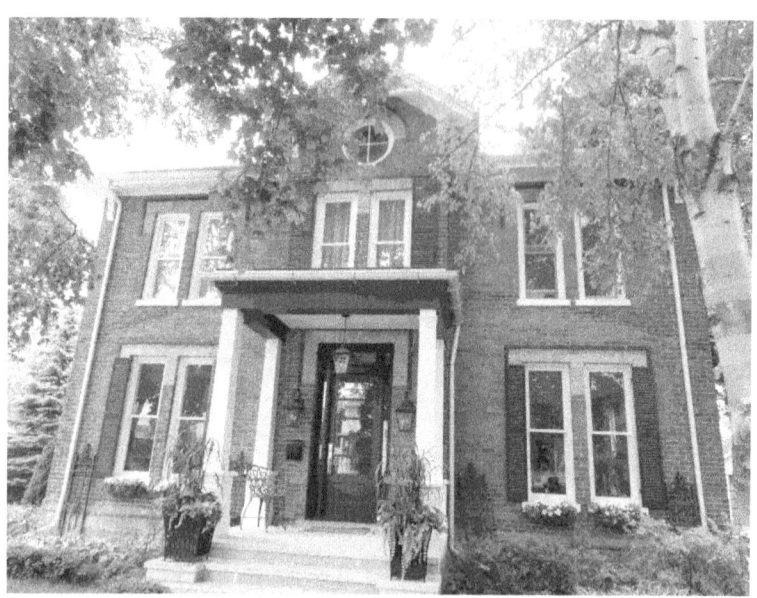

Italianate style with frontispiece with square pillars, decorated gable

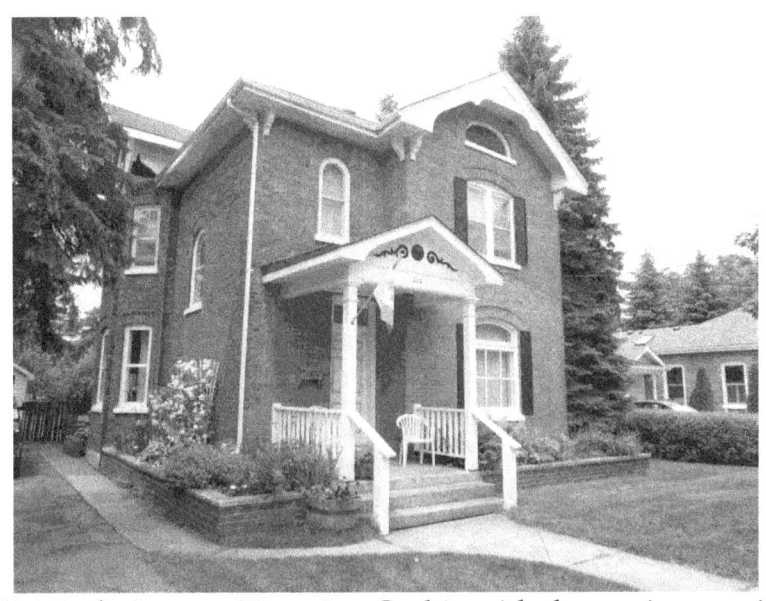

252 Maple Street – Victorian Gothic with decorative cornice brackets, Vergeboard on gables

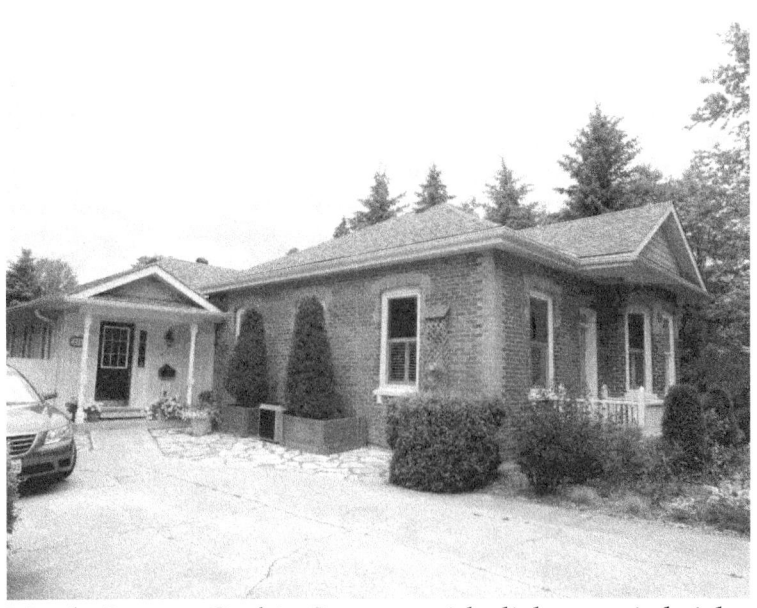

224 Maple Street - Gothic Cottage with dichromatic brickwork

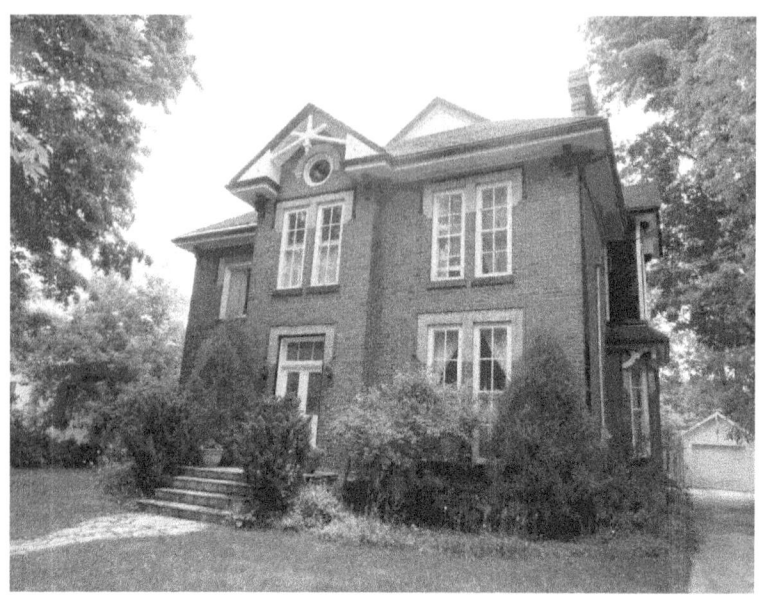

Italianate with decorative frontispiece, buff-coloured window hoods

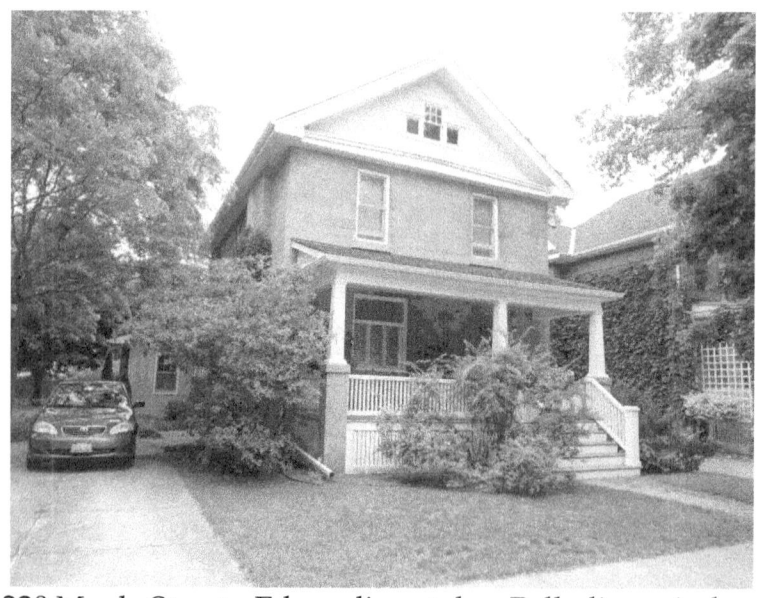

220 Maple Street - Edwardian style – Palladian window

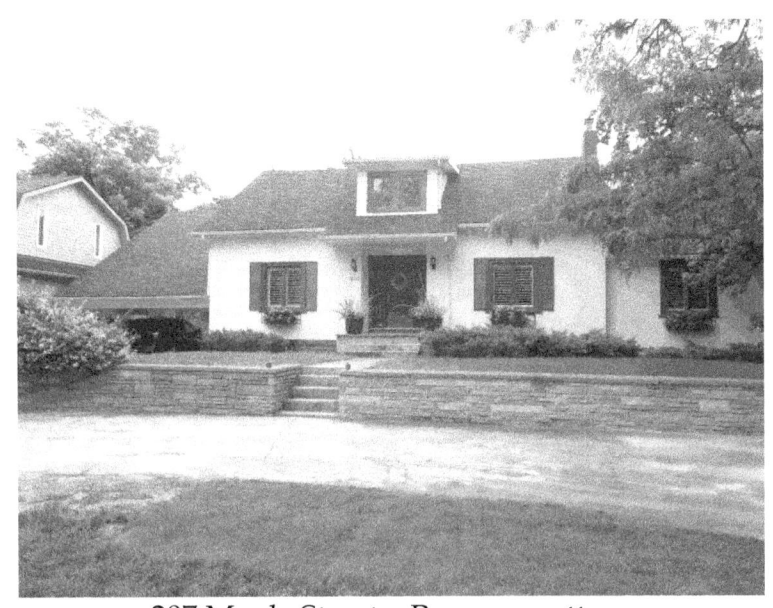

207 Maple Street – Regency cottage

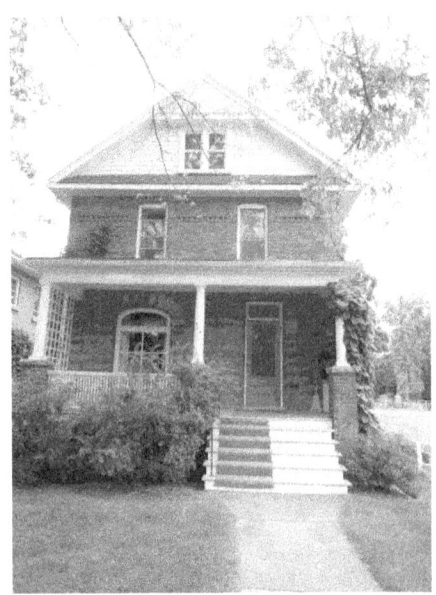

204 Maple Street – Edwardian style

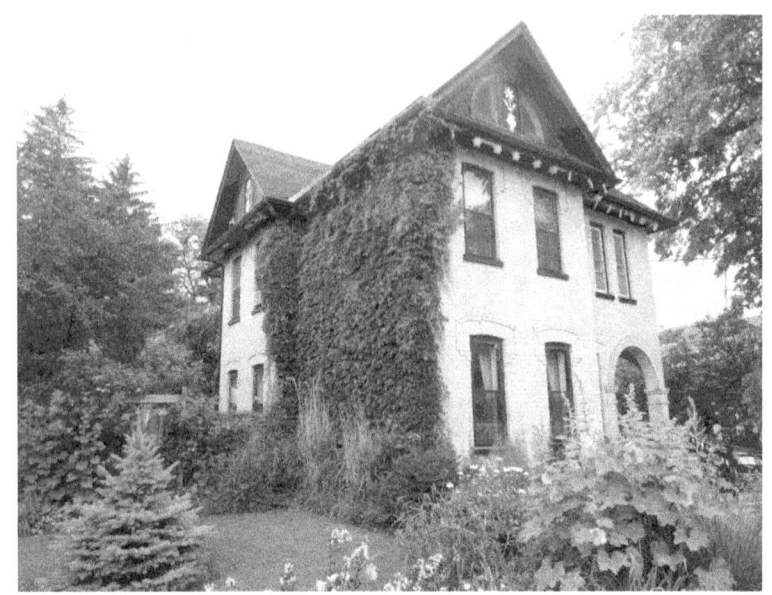

162 Maple Street - Gothic Revival – yellow brick, decorated tympanum, round arch, decorative window hoods

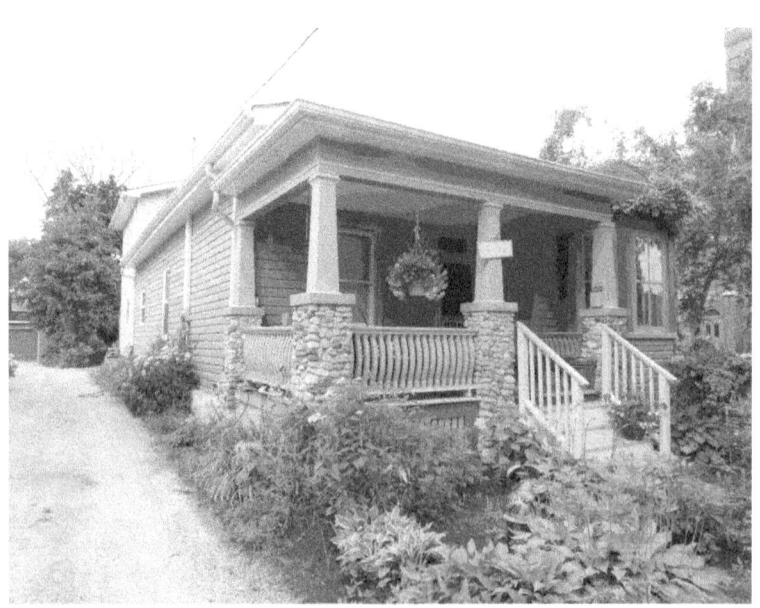

Regency Cottage – 148 Maple Street

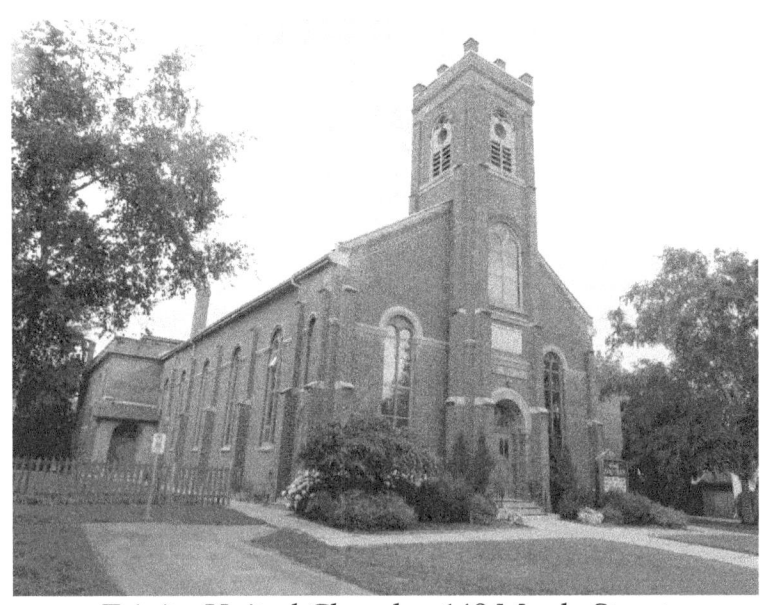

Trinity United Church – 140 Maple Street – cornerstone laid in 1863 (Maple Street Methodist)

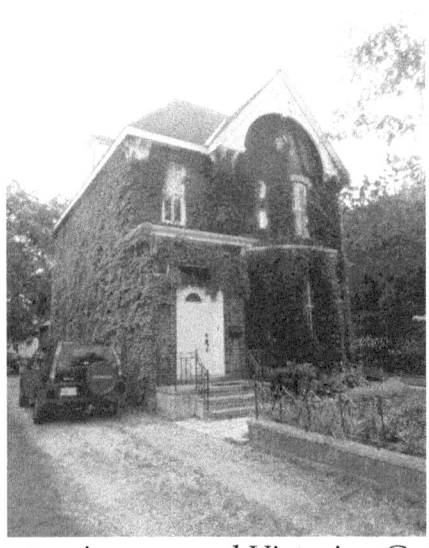

125 Maple Street - vine covered Victorian Gothic/Italianate style

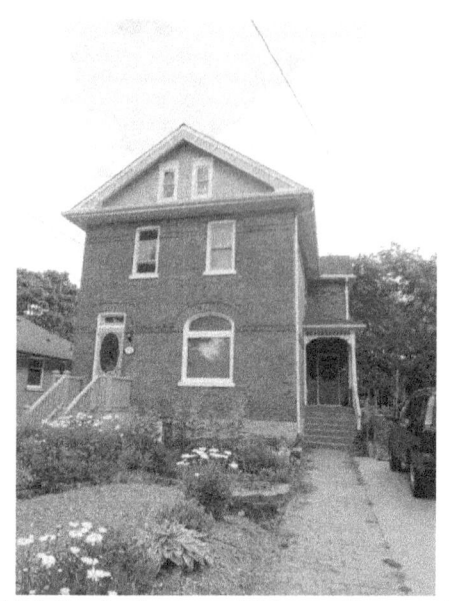

119 Maple Street – Edwardian style

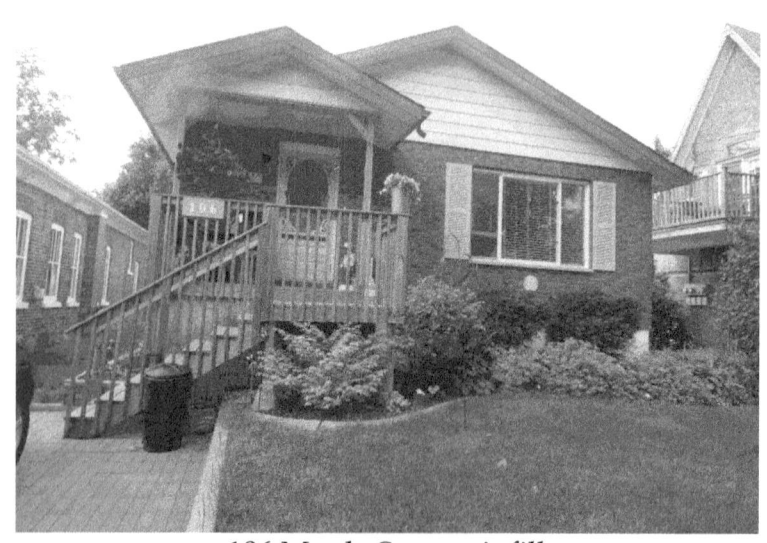

106 Maple Street - infill

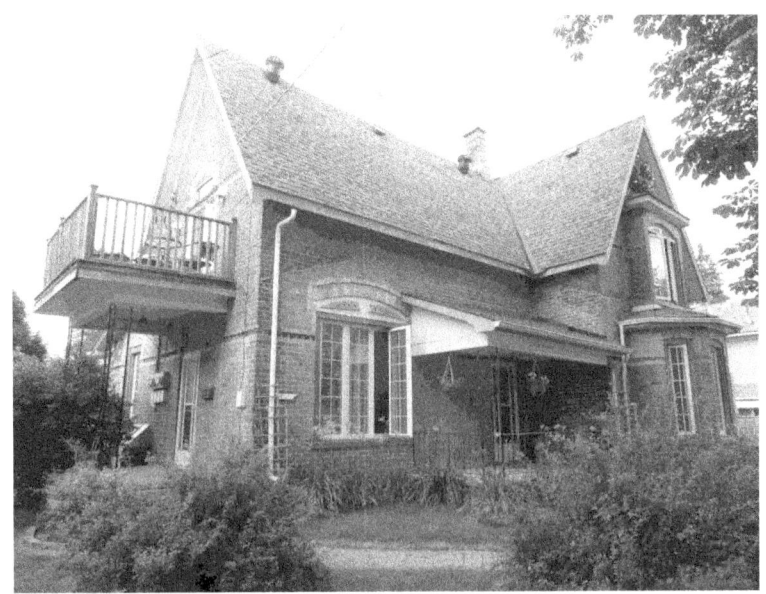

102 Maple Street – Gothic Revival – decorative arched window hoods, two storey bay window

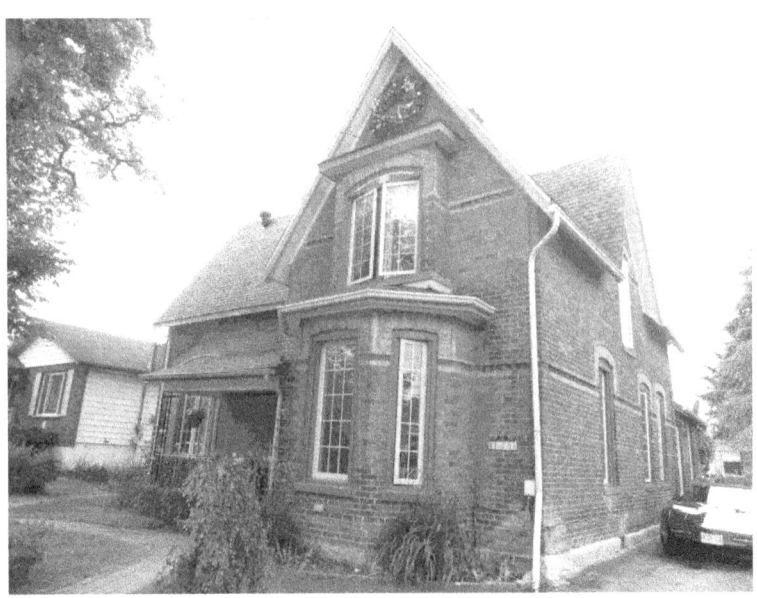

100 Maple Street

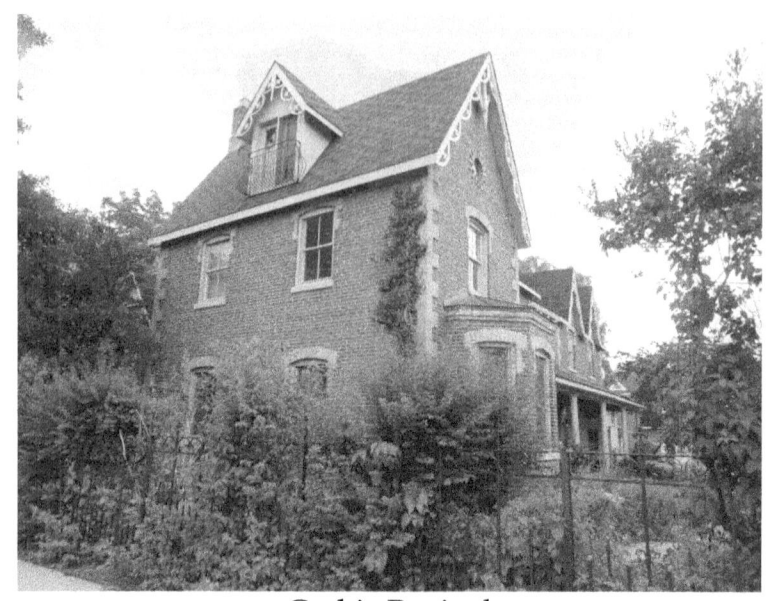

Gothic Revival
93 Maple Street

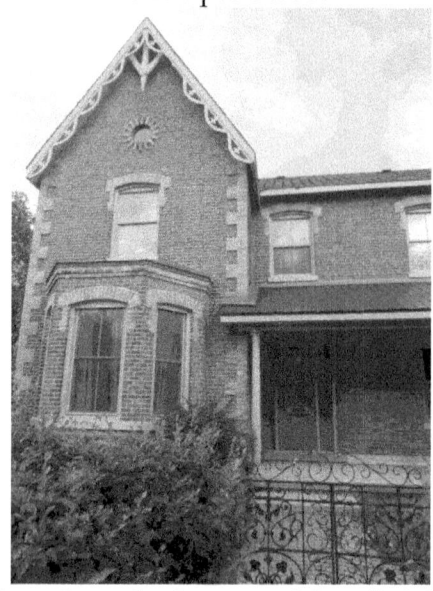

Decorative Vergeboard trim on gables, finial, dichromatic brickwork

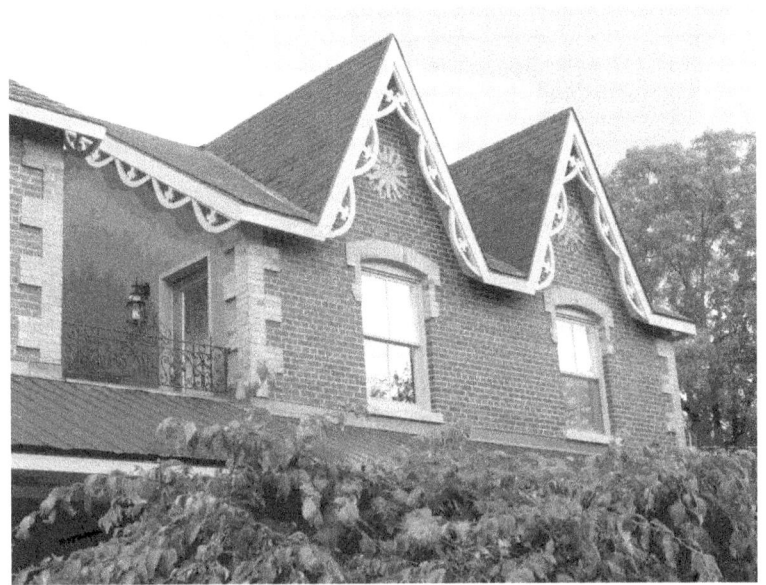

93 Maple Street

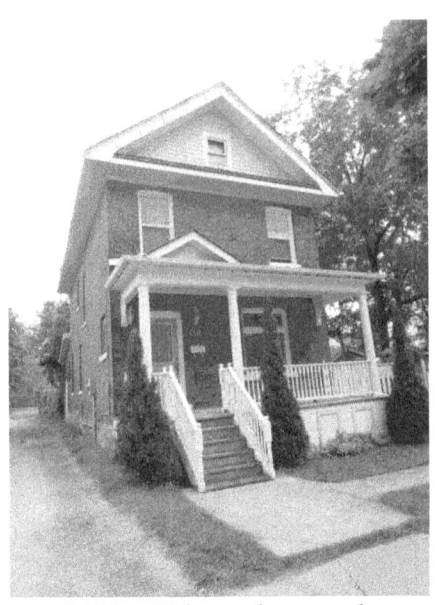

#130 – Edwardian style

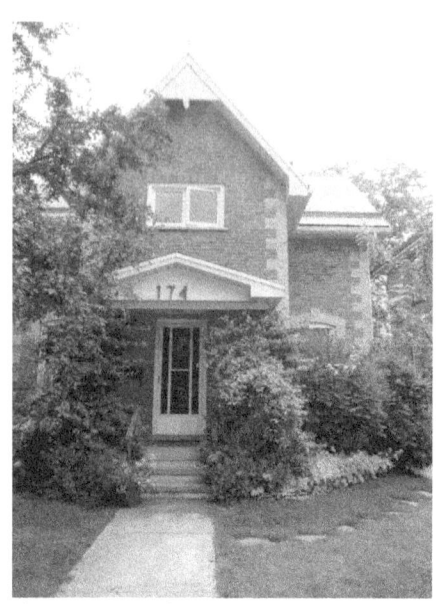

#174 – Gothic Revival with dichromatic brickwork

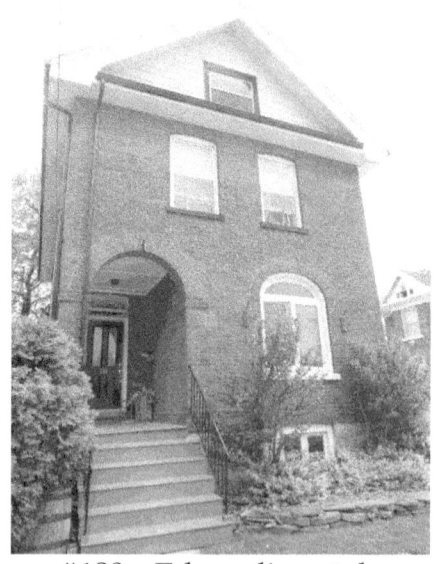

#180 – Edwardian style

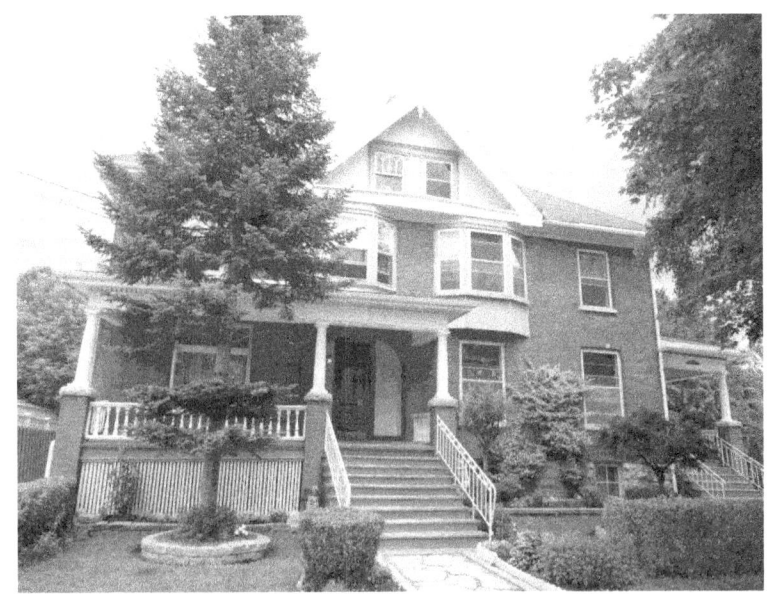

#175 – Vergeboard trim and finial on gable, deep porches

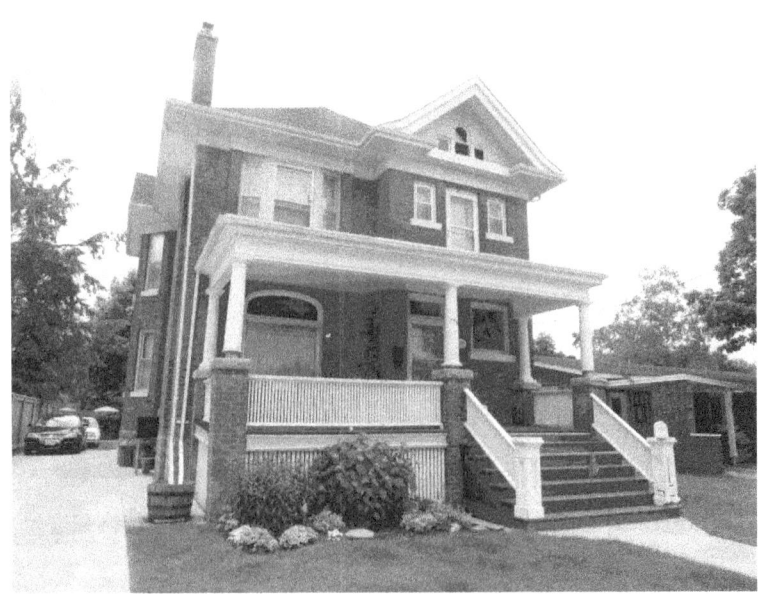

#190 – Italianate with Palladian window in attic gable

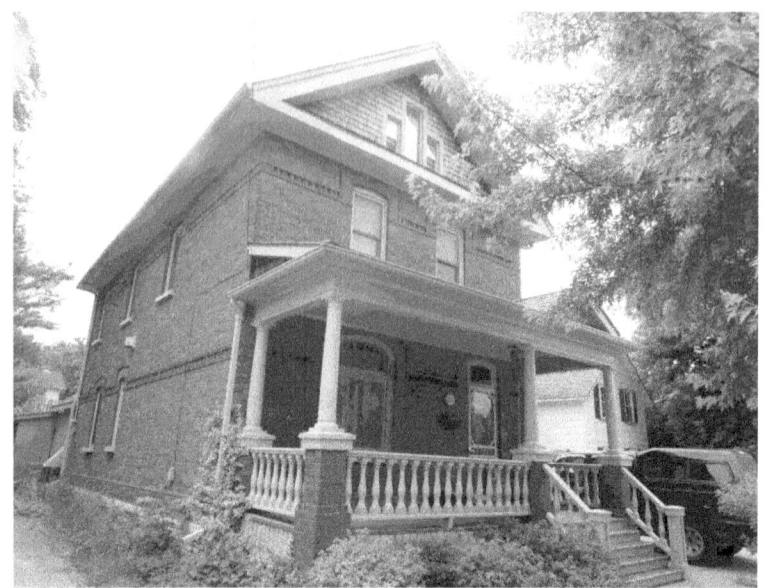
#224 - Edwardian style with Palladian window in gable

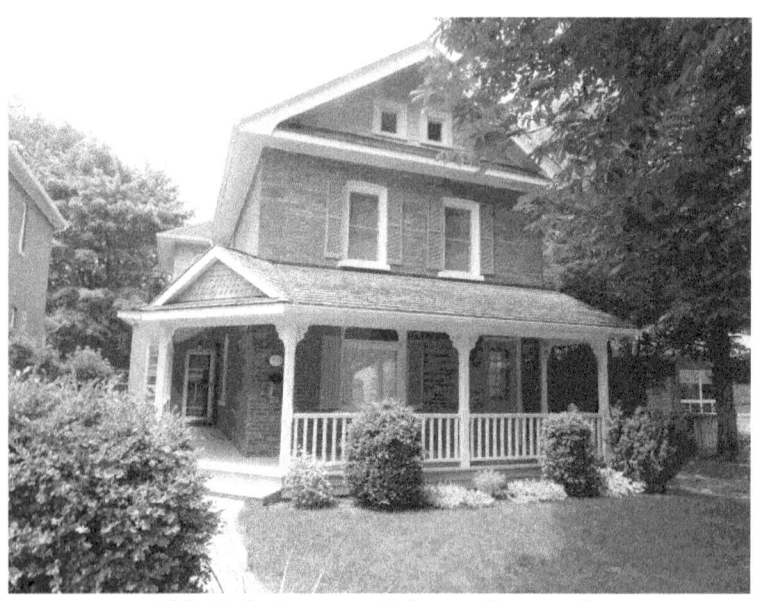
130 Oak Street – Edwardian style

Architectural Terms

Brackets: a decorative or weight-bearing structural element which forms a right angle with one side against a wall and the other under a projecting surface such as an eave or roof.	
Buttress: a masonry structure built against or projecting from a wall which serves to support or reinforce the wall. In Canadian architecture, they are sometimes used for decoration. Example: 200 Maple Street	
Cornice: originally the wooden overhand of the roof. With the use of stone, brick, iron and steel, the cornice is any projecting shelf at the top of a ceiling or roof. They can be very decorative.	
Dentil Moulding: an even series of rectangles used as ornamental decoration in cornices. Example: Downtown building facade	
Dichromatic brickwork: the use of two colours of brick, tile or slate to decorate a façade. Example: Downtown building facade	
Dormer: (French for "sleep") a gable end window that pierces through the plane of a sloping roof surface to create usable space in the top floor or attic of a building by adding headroom. Example: 80 Third Street	
Finial: ornament added to the top of a gable, pinnacle, canopy or spire – a Gothic element. Example: 242 Pine Street	

Frontispiece: a portion of the façade of a building, usually a centred doorway, that is slightly raised from the rest of the building, usually with white columned porches. Example: 203 Pine Street	
Gable: the triangular portion of a wall between the edges of a sloping roof. Example: 258 Pine Street	
Hipped Roof: a roof where all sides slope downwards to the walls with no gables.	
Keystones and Voussoirs: a voussoir is a wedge-shaped element used in building an arch. A keystone is the central stone that locks all the stones into position, allowing the arch to bear weight. A keystone is often enlarged and embellished. Example: 299 Maple Street	
Lancet Window: a tall, narrow window with a pointed arch at its top. Example: 200 Maple Street	
Palladian Window: a large window that is divided into three sections with the centre section larger than the two side sections and usually arched.	
Pediment: a triangular section above the horizontal structure (entablature), typically supported by columns. The inside of the triangle is called the tympanum. 203 Pine St.	

Quoin: masonry blocks at the corner of a wall, often a decorative feature, usually larger or of a different colour than the rest of the wall. Example: Downtown building facade	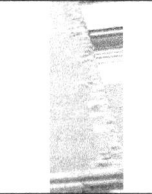
Vergeboards: also called bargeboards – hang from the projecting end of a roof and are often elaborately carved and ornamented. Example: 93 Maple Street	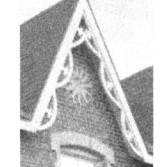

Collingwood's Building Styles

Georgian, before 1860 – These buildings have balanced facades around a central door, medium-pitched gable roofs, and small paned windows. Example: 258 Maple Street	
Regency Cottage, 1830-1860 – This style is a modest one-storey house with a low-pitched hip roof and has a symmetrical front façade. Example: 87 Third Street	
Gothic Revival, 1830-1890 – These decorative buildings have sharply-pitched gables with highly detailed vergeboards, pointed-arch window openings, and dichromatic brickwork, a common style in Ontario. Examples: 93 Maple Street	
Italianate, 1850-1900 – It has wide-bracketed eaves, belvederes, wrap-around verandahs. Examples: 203 Pine Street	
Queen Anne, 1885-1900 – This style has an irregular outline with a combination of an offset tower, broad gables, projecting two-storey bays, verandahs, multi-sloped roofs, and tall, decorative chimneys. Example: 200 Oak Street	
Edwardian, 1900-1930 – This style bridges the ornate and elaborate styles of the Victorian era and the simplified styles of the 20th century, with balanced facades, simple roof lines, dormer windows, large front porches, and smooth brick surfaces. Example: 202 Pine St.	

www.ingramcontent.com/pod-product-compliance
Lightning Source LLC
Chambersburg PA
CBHW071810170526
45167CB00003B/1255